THE CRUCIBLE OF ISLAM

THE CRUCIBLE OF ISLAM

G. W. Bowersock

Harvard University Press
Cambridge, Massachusetts, and London, England

Printed in the United States of America

First Harvard University Press paperback edition, 2019
First printing

Library of Congress Cataloging-in-Publication Data

Names: Bowersock, G. W. (Glen Warren), 1936– author.
Title: The crucible of Islam / G. W. Bowersock.
Description: Cambridge, Massachusetts : Harvard University Press, 2017. | Includes bibliographical references and index.
Identifiers: LCCN 2016046008 |
ISBN 9780674057760 (cloth : alk. paper) |
ISBN 9780674237728 (pbk.)
Subjects: LCSH: Islam—History. | Arabs—History—To 622. |
Islamic Empire—History—622–661.
Classification: LCC BP50 .B69 2017 | DDC 297.09/021—dc23
LC record available at https://lccn.loc.gov/2016046008

CONTENTS

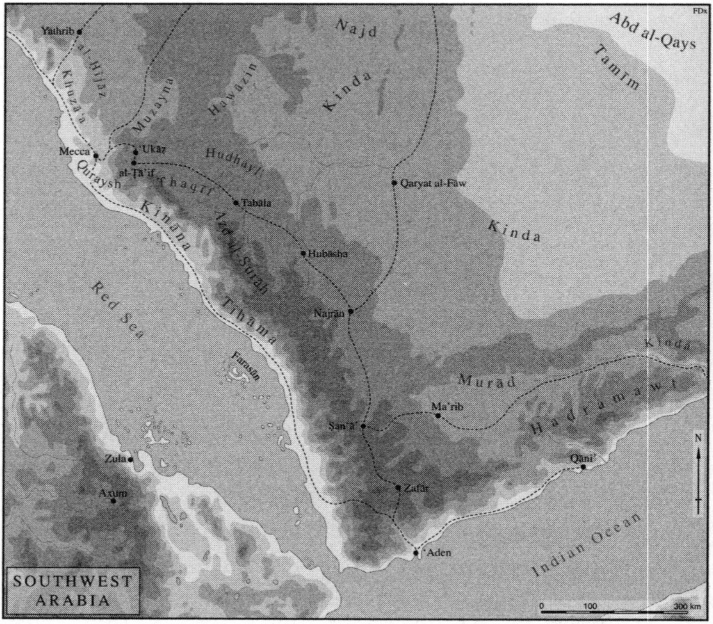

Map of Southwest Arabia, prepared by Fabrice Delrieux.

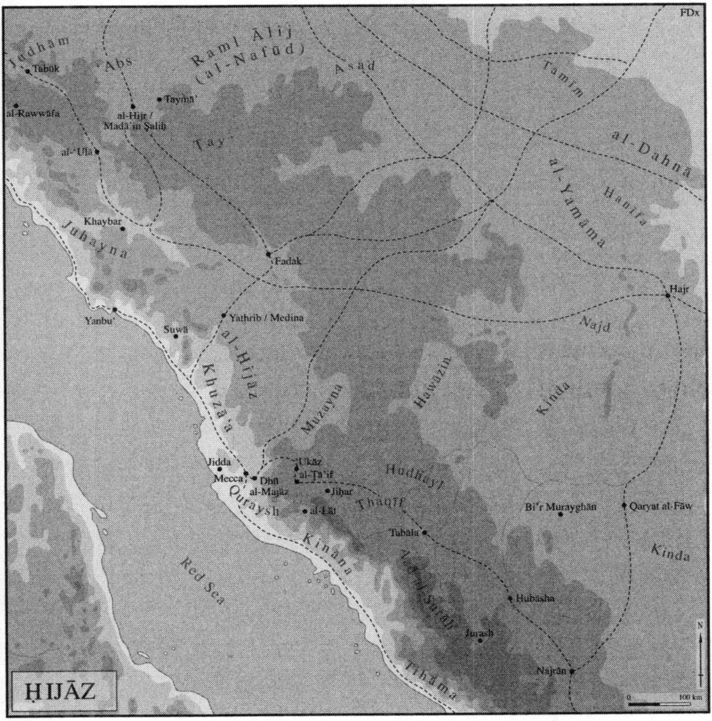

Map of the Ḥijāz, prepared by Fabrice Delrieux.

THE CRUCIBLE OF ISLAM

PROLOGUE

THE FAITH THAT drove the armies of Arabs out of the Arabian peninsula to take possession of Palestine, North Africa, and Syria within a few decades in the first half of the seventh century remains today a powerful force in world affairs. What generated this force is as obscure now as it was in the beginning, and historians have been impeded by the tendentious character of most of the sources for this great upheaval, as well as by their own prejudices. It is difficult for non-Muslims, above all Jews and Christians, to be dispassionate in confronting the tide of Muslim conquests that swept over the ancient cultures of the Near East. It is no less difficult for Muslims to apply scholarly rigor to the word of God as well as to a historiographical tradition that significantly post-dates the events it records. Yet in view of the immense authority of Islam in the modern world it becomes more imperative than ever for both sides to make the effort.

The pioneering generation of Islamicists in the West, including Theodor Nöldeke, Julius Wellhausen, and Ignaz Goldziher, applied the methods of classical philology as they had been successfully imported into the study of the New Testament and the Hebrew Bible by Erasmus and Gesenius. As these scholars recognized, the transmission of these old texts was susceptible to critical analysis, which in the fullness of time could be supplemented by surviving documents on stone, papyri, and coins, and eventually the discoveries of archaeological excavation. For Islam the authority of the Qur'ān, being the revealed word of God, notoriously resisted the Erasmian challenge, because of the vast hiatus between its creation, at whatever time and by whatever means, and very much later reports of the context from which it came. It took nearly two centuries for Islamic exegetes to acquire a corpus of what was known about the genesis of their religion. By then a complex process of textual contamination was already in place. During those two centuries non-Muslim chroniclers, interpreters, and historians had been at work in a variety of languages—Greek, Latin, Armenian, Syriac, and Arabic above all. They had conspicuously exploited one another's material, which left traces of their borrowing in the texts they wrote, but naturally they had their own doctrinal perspectives.

Three recent books illustrate the dilemma facing anyone looking into the crucible in which Islam was forged.[1] Although there is little doubt that this crucible lay in the northwestern Arabian peninsula, contacts between that region and the surrounding cultures of Palestine, Himyar, Ethiopia, and Persia inevitably contributed to a potentially explosive mixture. So did indigenous traditions of polytheism that had been there all along, as well as a more recent evolution of Jewish and Christian communities that was replete with hostility and massacre. The three new books attempt to examine the rise of Islam in very different ways. Yet they all traverse the familiar path that starts the rise of Islam with Muḥammad's birth at Mecca about 570 and the revelations he received from Gabriel, and they then progress to his subsequent emigration *(hijra)* to Medina in 622. They all continue with a series of traditional dates, battles, and conquests. All three books record Muḥammad's canonical death in 632 and go on to examine the turbulent reigns of the four so-called orthodox caliphs who succeeded him before the establishment of the Umayyad dynasty in Damascus about 661.[2] By their very diversity, these three accounts of the rise of Islam illustrate the problems inherent in telling this story.

Fred Donner, in his *Muhammad and the Believers,* explains what happened in an essentially chronological narrative that commingles quotations from the Qur'ān and various early documents with testimony from the traditional Muslim sources of several centuries later. He consciously writes with an eye to providing a generally sympathetic and generous view of the early Muslims that might be acceptable in the fraught politics of today. Hence his insistence on calling them "the Believers," which is, to be sure, a perfectly correct rendering of the term that was often used for the followers of Muḥammad. He thinks that the community of Believers was considerably more ecumenical than many other historians have thought and that it was both open to contact with Jews and Christians and receptive of their views. Readers have been quick to notice that Donner's account of Islamic origins portrayed a first generation of Muslims who seem much less menacing than they appeared to the Jews and Christians at the time, or to most historians since. But he does not avoid the many divisive and sanguinary encounters that the Believers had with others and even with many of their own.

In his history of the Arab conquest and the creation of an Islamic empire, *In God's Path,* Robert Hoyland has reasonably adopted an approach that largely rejects treating later and tendentious texts as sources for the formative age of Islam. These are not only Arabic texts of the *ḥadīth,* but equally Arabic historiography (above all al-Ṭabarī), Arabic Christian historiography (such as Agapius), numerous Syriac chronicles, and Greek histories such as the vast *Chronographia* of Theophanes Confessor, who relied upon sources now lost that were themselves dependent upon sources that were already lost when he was writing. Because Muslim historical sources are missing until the ninth century, Hoyland chose to confine himself to those extant texts that came only from the first two centuries of the Islamic era. Their authority would accordingly derive from their closeness to the events they describe.

But this is a risky methodology. These are inevitably Christian and Jewish sources, which are close to the events they describe but more directly colored by them. They tend to display a predictable undercurrent of antipathy to the Muslims. Hoyland compensates for this weakness by adroitly turning to the peripheral nations that impinged upon Muslim territory. In this way he gains a broader perspective for the events of the period. Hence he looks farther afield to Georgia, Armenia, and Central Asia, and by comparison can track whatever malice or error the contemporary or near-contemporary writers in the Near East itself might have been inspired to import into their narratives.

The great peril in Hoyland's approach is the potential loss of genuinely illuminating information that might lurk in those later Muslim accounts. A historian must always be alert to the tendentiousness of sources but is not always justified in discarding them altogether. What is required is a meticulous examination of multiple tellings of the same story in an effort to determine its outlines as well as the deformations to which it has been subjected. This is exactly what Maria Conterno has done, in exemplary fashion, in her analysis of the sources that lay behind the narrative of Theophanes for the two centuries before his time.[3]

By far the longest, most searching, and most thoroughly documented account of these early years has come in the third of the recent books on the rise of Islam. That is Aziz al-Azmeh's *The Emergence of Islam in Late Antiquity,* a work that for its immense range and profundity has no equal in modern scholarship. Unlike Donner and Hoyland, he does not attempt to provide a narrative of the rise of Islam, but rather to delineate the entire culture in which it emerged. Al-Azmeh unfolds his argument in a dense and often theoretical prose, but he knows what he is doing. Above all he knows the Arabic sources intimately, and he is able to bring to them an exceptional knowledge of Greek such as few Arabists now possess. This was not always so, of course, because Arabic philology in the West was rooted in classical philology. One of the greatest of the pioneers was Johann Jakob Reiske in the eighteenth century, whose contributions to textual criticism in Greek (Libanius) and Arabic (Abu'l fida) endure undiminished to this day.

Al-Azmeh can move between later Muslim witnesses and the earlier Christian and Jewish ones with unusual precision. He pays due attention to the periphery, though not so assiduously as Hoyland, but he systematically mines the Muslim traditions at the same time as directing his attention to new epigraphical discoveries in various Semitic scripts and languages, as well as to archaeological excavations in the territory of early Islam. His attempt to rename the early Islamic period as Paleo-Islam will probably not succeed in altering current usage, but what he detects in that age is undoubtedly something very different from the picture that has been traditionally retrojected into the period by western European, Byzantine, and Muslim historians, who have so often worked in isolation.

Both Hoyland and al-Azmeh, despite their different styles and approaches, recognize that there is a disquieting emptiness in much of what we know about the Arabs and their religion between approximately 560 and 660. Yet these hundred years constitute precisely the chronological frame within which momentous events that changed the course of world history actually took place. The years that introduce and conclude the central epoch of this story are notoriously obscure and make it difficult for a historian to gain a proper perspective on that central epoch—an epoch that comprises the revelations to the Prophet Muḥammad from 610 onward, through his eventual emigration to Medina, and then his first wars of conquest down to his death in 632. For Arabia and the origins of Islam, the years from 560 to 610 and from 632 to 660 are particularly muddy. It is difficult to gain a clear view of Arabian society at the time when Muḥammad came into the world, and although the era of conquest is better recorded in the Islamic tradition, the final phase of this obscure epoch embraces all four caliphs who succeeded

Muḥammad before the establishment of the Umayyad dynasty in Damascus.

The pages that follow are not intended to be another narrative of the rise of Islam, but to provide a glimpse into the chaotic environment that made Islam possible, and ideally to help in understanding how it was formed. This was an environment that had absorbed into its own native Arabian culture a series of external influences that reflected the milieu in which Arabia was situated—Ethiopia, Palestine, the Byzantine Empire, and Sassanian Persia.

The relative emptiness of the years 560 to 610 is relieved by a surge of activity among the Sassanian Persians that began with the death of the Byzantine emperor Maurice in 602. The Persians detected an opportunity for renewed conquest in opposition to the new government in Constantinople, and this enabled them to capture Jerusalem in 614. But before the death of Maurice, there is an alarming gap in historical information for the Near East generally, and in particular for Arabia. The gap is alarming above all because it was precisely during this period that Muḥammad is said to have been born. We possess tolerably good documentation for the western and southwestern parts of the Arabian peninsula in the middle of the sixth century, during the years when the Ethiopian Christian Abraha dominated the region. He even launched a campaign into the region of Mecca, which, as we will see, may or may not be reflected in the Qur'ān. But after Abraha's death and the unsuccessful efforts of his heirs to hold onto his power, the Persians took control at some point in the vicinity of 570, and our knowledge becomes tenuous and imprecise. Yet this just happens to be the traditional date for Muḥammad's birth. From that point our information dries up until the death of Maurice.

As for the four caliphs who succeeded Muḥammad after his death in 632, they are known as the orthodox *(rāshidūn)* caliphs and, to a greater or lesser degree, they came from the inner circle of the new faith. But these rulers presided over a time of great uncertainty, as can be seen at once from the fact that all but the first were murdered. The four were the Prophet's father-in-law, Abū Bakr (632–634), ʻUmar ibn al-Khaṭṭāb (634–644), ʻUthmān ibn Affān (644–656), and the Prophet's cousin ʻAlī (656–661). This bare outline of a troubled age is testimony enough to the instability of a period that later Muslim tradition came to look back upon respectfully as a golden age. That was only because out of that instability the Muslims managed to conquer Palestine, Syria, and North Africa and to create the template for the first Islamic dynasty, which began with the Umayyads in 661. The subsequent refashioning of this uneasy time, which ended with the first of two civil wars, must serve as a warning against uncritical acceptance of the traditions emanating from that later time, but it does not altogether indict them as unworthy of attention. It simply reminds the historian to be constantly alert, as much to the preservation of embedded authentic material as to misrepresentation.

The stormy years of the *rāshidūn* are at least visible to us through the traditions about the early Muslims. The wars of apostasy *(ridda)* began immediately after Muḥammad's death, and the first civil war brought the orthodox era to a close, when the Umayyad dynasty took hold in Damascus in 661. Even so, uncertainty reigns about exactly when and how the text of Islam's holy book was codified, and how it was disseminated. The traditional view that ʻUthmān supervised a controlled redaction has recently come under scrutiny through the discovery of an early palimpsest in Ṣanʻā', and even what were long thought to be the earliest citations of Quranic texts, those on the Dome of the Rock in Jerusalem, are not consistent with the canonical version.[4]

So the crucible of Islam remains an elusive vessel. Although it may never be possible to describe it in definitive detail, an attempt to delineate its principal contours and the molten ingredients that it contained will oblige us to step aside both from unquestioning acceptance of later Muslim tradition and equally unquestioning rejection of it. We have also to step aside from rigid adherence to those non-Muslim witnesses that were closer to the events they report, simply because they came earlier. Rigid methodologies have run their course by now. A classical scholar and ancient historian, such as the present writer, may perhaps be allowed to say that the factional quarrels that have bedeviled Western scholarship on early Islam should be brought to a close. This is not the place to renew those quarrels. Minimalism is not the way to throw light on a dark age. Interpreting the Qur'ān exclusively by reference to its text without invoking outside or later sources is injudicious and unhistorical, even if it makes a scholar's life easier or even seems superficially plausible. Similarly, reading only Jewish and Christian texts about the origins of Islam, because the Islamic texts came later, cannot dispense a historian from asking what the Arabs were thinking and saying precisely when those earlier texts were being written. To whom did those non-Muslim writers talk? What texts were they reading, and in what languages? Jews certainly interacted with Arabs, just as Christians did. If a Christian writing about Arabs in Syriac quoted Greek in transliteration, where did he get it? If John of Damascus cited specific chapters (suras) of the Qur'ān in his Greek rhetoric, how did he know about them?[5]

What follows is an attempt to expose and describe the complex cultural and social environment that fostered a new religion precisely where Judaism, Christianity, and ancient pagan cults had endured for centuries. It is an attempt that does not depend upon any single methodology, but, in the old classical tradition of Richard Bentley, invokes as often as possible critical reasoning in confrontation with whatever is transmitted, rightly or wrongly, as fact: *ratio et res ipsa.*

1

THE ARABIAN KINGDOM OF ABRAHA

THE WESTERN PART of the Arabian peninsula, extending southward from ʿAqaba to the Indian Ocean, lay in the midst of a network of international power and trade. The territory of the Ḥijāz in the northwest corner, the low-lying strip of Tihāma along the western coast, the interior plateau of Najd with the oasis of al-Yamāma to the east, and Ḥimyar to the south, roughly encompassing modern Yemen, all faced a formidable array of powers on every side. These were, above all, Byzantium, which controlled Palestine and Syria to the north, and Sassanian Persia, which dominated Mesopotamia and Iran to the northeast. But there was also international commerce, originating and terminating in the Red Sea to the west. Its traders sailed in the Indian Ocean between the Persian Gulf on the eastern side of the Arabian peninsula and ports on the Egyptian and Ethiopian coast, and this meant that the two competing empires could not ignore the economic role of Arabia. Even before the opening up of commercial routes by sea in the Hellenistic period, western Arabia had provided overland routes through which the perfumes and spices of the Ḥaḍramawt made their way northward into Transjordan and Syria and westward to the Mediterranean.

The whole region was rich in history and traditions. Before either the Byzantines or the Sassanians, the Romans had endeavored to keep watch on what was happening there. Under the Antonine emperors they had set up a military garrison in the Farasān islands, off the western Arabian coast in the Red Sea, clearly to ensure that commercial links between Arabia and Egypt were kept open.[1] The Ḥijāz in the north had once constituted the lower part of the old Nabataean kingdom, with its city of tombs at Madā'in Ṣāliḥ, which was a kind of lesser Petra, and it was only natural for the whole area to be incorporated into the province of Arabia that Trajan created out of the Nabataean kingdom. Farther south in the interior, an indigenous kingdom of the Ḥujrid tribe of Kinda had spawned an influential settlement at Qaryat al-Fāw, where sculpture and wall paintings revealed bold appropriations of Greek models.[2] At the same time at Yathrib, Jewish settlers, who may have entered the peninsula in the aftermath of the revolt against Titus in Jerusalem, built up communities that eventually rivaled those of the tribe of the Quraysh, who were in charge at Mecca to the south. Still further south, a vigorous Christian community at Najrān was proof of the spread of Byzantium's state religion into one of the key peripheral territories outside its empire.

The Ethiopians at Axum had occupied Ḥimyar in Southwest Arabia during the early third century when they were still pagans, possibly in response to rivalries that the Antonine garrison at Farasān had been designed to forestall. Inexplicably the same Ethiopians withdrew after a little less than a hundred years and retreated to their capital in the Horn of Africa. But their departure left the region prey to aggressive Arab tribes that converted to Judaism in the late fourth century and established a kingdom of their own in Ḥimyar.[3] The adoption of Judaism and the name of Israel may have been the outcome of an all but invisible spread of monotheism earlier in the fourth century from Jewish settlements in the peninsula. But by an astonishing coincidence this dramatic development occurred just as the Ethiopians on the other side of the Red Sea were abandoning their old gods and converting to Christianity.[4] Not surprisingly the young Byzantine empire, based in Constantinople, and the somewhat older Persian empire of the Sassanians, whose capital was at Ctesiphon in Mesopotamia, eyed with concern these transitions in Arabia because they conspicuously intersected their own zones of influence.

The tribal character of the Arabian people posed diplomatic problems for any large imperial government that had a vested interest in the economic, military, and religious potential of a complex society that lay so close to its frontiers. Byzantium made an effort to reinvigorate the old Roman system of client kings by working through its chosen Arab allies, the tribal confederation of the Ghassānids, more accurately called Jafnids, after their ruling dynasty, which was based at Jabala in southern Syria. The Persians countered by supporting clients of their own, another tribal confederation known as Lakhmids, but more accurately called Naṣrids, after a ruling dynasty that was located at al-Ḥīra, close to the border between Arabian and Persian territory.[5] A significant population of Christians in the Naṣrid capital might have been the descendants of earlier Jewish settlers, and the support of this community by the Zoroastrian

Persians reflected not only the international political imperatives of the time but the willingness of the leaders of divergent faiths to cooperate against a perceived common enemy.[6]

This kind of long-range diplomacy at the edges of Arabia was hardly sufficient to monitor, let alone control, the turbulent events of the remote and fragmented tribal societies both in the steppe and along the coast. When the Jewish kings of Ḥimyar began to persecute the Christians in their kingdom, this gave those Christian Ethiopians who nourished irredentist sympathies exactly the opportunity they needed to attempt to recover the southwest realm of the Arabian peninsula that they had abandoned several centuries before.

In AD 525 the reigning king of the Ethiopians at Axum, who bore the local title of *negus,* decided to invade Ḥimyar after taking the biblical name of Kālēb in addition to his birth name of Ella Asbeha. This momentous enterprise represented the culmination of his claims to rule over much of Yemen, much as his ancestors had several centuries earlier. His decision sprang from a deep irredentist strain in Ethiopian culture that looked to occupying southwestern Arabia. By his invasion Kālēb succeeded in annihilating the Jewish regime that been associated with a fanatical ruler Joseph (Yūsuf), who had launched a massacre of Christians at Najrān in 523. This horrifying event had served as justification for the Ethiopians' invasion.[7] The Byzantine emperor played a role in encouraging the *negus,* even though the Ethiopians' Monophysite Christianity was different from Byzantium's Chalcedonian orthodoxy.

Kālēb's victory in Ḥimyar brought a definitive end to Ḥimyarite Judaism and replaced it with Christianity. In the region the Ethiopians installed a new ruler of their own, Sumyafa 'Ashwa'. But he did not last long, and, after a brief period of uncertainty, an Ethiopian general by the name of Abraha, who reportedly came from a servile background in the port city of Adulis, arose from the ranks of the occupying army as the new Christian Ethiopian king of Ḥimyar, and he clearly had no desire to be a surrogate for Kālēb.[8] The Ethiopian soldiers in Arabia much preferred the agreeable coastal climate of Yemen to their homeland, and that is presumably why they opted to elevate one of their own and stand by him. Although Kālēb had clearly expected Abraha to be his surrogate in Arabia, it turned out that the new ruler had far more ambitious plans of his own. He declined to act as a puppet of the Axumite government and proceeded to govern independently and forcefully for several decades.[9]

Abraha then greedily assumed the whole range of titles that the kings of Ḥimyar had displayed in the past, titles to which the Ethiopian rulers had long aspired even when they had no legitimate claim to them. Abraha's titulature was an explicit realization of Ethiopian irredentism in the Arabian peninsula. He proudly declared himself king of Saba, dhū-Raydān, Ḥaḍramawt, Yamanat, and the nomadic Arabs of Tawd and Tihāma. But the title he actually bore as ruler is less clear. He was, in the usual understanding of the Sabaic words that stand on a magnificent inscribed stele of 547, a "viceroy" *(ʿzly)*, or "deputy-king," but for someone as proud and active as Abraha this does not seem very plausible. It makes much more sense to interpret the word *ʿzly* followed by *mlk*^{n} *ʾgʿzy*^{n} as a way of showing that he was a ruler who held the title of king. He was equipped with an equally puzzling epithet, *Rmḥs*^{3}, which has been well explained as meaning "courageous" by comparison with Arabic words deriving from "lance" or "spear," although less plausible interpretations, such as a form of the Greek *Rhōmaios,* have also been proposed.[10] But Procopius's report that Abraha was the ex-slave of a Byzantine trader hardly deserves that much credibility.[11]

Abraha's refusal to be a surrogate for the Ethiopian *negus* in Axum had accorded well with the desires of the Ethiopian soldiery that had refused to go back home. Whether Kālēb died or retreated to a monastery, there is no doubt that Abraha was left to manage his Arabian kingdom on his own, and he set about making major changes that buttressed the religion he established in the region.

The Ethiopian conquest of Ḥimyar marked the end of Judaism as a state religion, and the Christianity that replaced it seems to have been closely allied to traditions in northwest Arabia that were strongly influenced by Syriac. The inscriptions of Abraha differ strikingly from those of his short-lived predecessor in their use of Syriac borrowings for Christian terms, such as *ruḥ* for Spirit as opposed to Ethiopic *manfas,* and conspicuously in the Aramaic borrowing in Sabaic *byt* for church. The Greek *ekklēsia,* from Hellenic Christianity, is also incorporated in the name of Abraha's great church at Ṣan'ā', al-Qalīs, with a name formed directly from the consonants of the Greek word.[12] The implication of this language is that the Ethiopian imposition of Christianity in Ḥimyar did not entail the imposition of Ethiopian Christianity. It evidently served to reinvigorate the Christianity that was already there and had survived in the region for several centuries. This presumably meant that it need not have been Monophysite (non-Chalcedonian) and may well explain Byzantine support for the new government.

The rule of Abraha was a time of great consolidation in Ḥimyar, with the building of churches and a famous repair of the great dam, which had burst in the city of Mārib. To signal his role on the international diplomatic stage, Abraha convoked a great conference in that very city in 547, precisely when the dam had burst and required repair, and he commemorated this conference and the repair of the dam in a magnificent inscription.[13] He brought together the leaders of the most powerful nations in the eastern Mediterranean at that time. These included delegates from Constantinople and Ctesiphon, who represented the two great empires that the Persian shah Khosroes would later describe in a letter to the Byzantine emperor Maurice as "the two eyes of the world."[14] Abraha also included representatives of the Jafnid clients of Byzantium, the Naṣrid clients of Persia, Justinian's Arab governor *(phylarch)* in Palestine, and the Ethiopian *negus* in Axum.

Abraha's church at Ṣan'ā' was one of the wonders of Arabia, and the Arabic tradition reports that stones and marble had been transported from the palace at Mārib to be incorporated in the great new building. Magnificent mosaics were adorned with crosses in

Inscription of Abraha from Mārib, *Corpus Inscriptionum Himyariticarum* 541, courtesy of Christian Julien Robin, Jeremy Schieccatte, and Laila Nehme.

silver and gold. The plan of the church appears to have been distinctly Syrian and may have been based upon the Church of the Holy Sepulchre in Jerusalem. The Arabic sources report that the emperor in Constantinople sent both marble and mosaics, as well as craftsmen to execute the work.[15] The church was clearly intended as a pilgrimage center, and hostels were set up to accommodate the pilgrims. Most remarkably, one of the Arab sources, the great history by al-Ṭabarī, suggests that the Qalīs was envisioned as a rival to the Kaʿba in Mecca for the tribes of Arabia. Such a direct competition with the supremacy of Mecca among Arab pagans would naturally have been unsettling to the custodians of the Kaʿba, the Quraysh of Mecca, and there is some reason to think that these people launched attacks against Christians and even attempted to profane the church in Sanʿā' with excrement.[16] Not many years would pass before Abraha himself undertook an expedition against Mecca.

But he had first to confront other opposition to his rule. Not long before he decided to convoke his international congress and ostentatiously repair the dam at Mārib, he had to deal with a revolt in the interior to the east. The leader was none other than Yazīd ibn Kabshat, from a branch of the tribe of Kinda, whom

Abraha had appointed as governor over the Kindites. It seems as if Yazīd was able to mobilize those local aristocrats who had formerly supported the Ḥimyarite Jews against the Ethiopians and saw an opportunity to regain their old authority. The revolt spread southward into the Ḥaḍramawt before Abraha's forces were able to drive the rebels back into Kinda. All this occurred, as we know from his large stele inscribed in 547, just as the dam burst in Mārib and the delegates of international potentates were about to confer at Abraha's invitation.[17] The various projects that occupied him in that year illustrate his shrewdness and energy. Nonetheless, we must beware of succumbing to the self-aggrandizement of this single inscription, because the epigraphy of his reign is scattered and not necessarily representative of any long-term imperial policy.

But fortunately chance finds have restored to history another great campaign that Abraha led only a few years later, in the early 550s. This time he marched north with his troops, rather than east and south, and he headed straight into the interior territory that lay on the way to Mecca. Inscriptions from Bi'r Murayghān, north of Najrān in central Arabia, record several expeditions, including one that Abraha led against the tribe of the Ma'add, which is described as the fourth incursion against this tribe.[18] It is quite possible that these four raids represented attempts to destabilize the Persian presence in central Arabia. Procopius, writing in the vicinity of 550, had written of Abraha's desire to weaken Persian influence, and the first inscription from Bi'r Murayghān records a settlement with a local prince called 'Amr, who was the son of a princess of Kinda and of al-Mundhir, the sheikh of Persia's Naṣrid clients. Abraha's campaign terminated in Ḥalibān, with his recognition of 'Amr as leader of the Ma'add in return for the delivery of 'Amr's son as a hostage.

At the same time, Abraha directed, through two of his generals, a campaign into the Ḥijāz to the northwest with troops drawn from four tribes in the region, including Kinda and Murād, which had fought against the Ethiopians in the past. This attack to the north, with armies from the four tribes advancing into the Ḥijāz not far from Mecca, reinforced Abraha's diplomatic initiative at Ḥalibān. It obviously strengthened his control far from his capital at Ṣan'ā' and put the Persians on notice that central Arabia was now his. The Quraysh in Mecca would have had reason to be concerned by the proximity of Abraha's armies in 552.

But the extent to which Abraha's campaigns may have left traces in subsequent Arabian tradition remains an open question. Some find an echo of the operations at Ḥalibān in pre-Islamic poetry.[19] More importantly, the miraculous repulse of an army led by an elephant on the way to Mecca has left a permanent record in Sura 105 of the Qur'ān: "Do you not see how the Lord dealt with the army of the Elephant? Did He not utterly confound their plans? He sent ranks of birds against them, pelting them with pellets of hard-baked clay." This defeat has sometimes been considered a foundational myth for Qurashi supremacy in western Arabia on the eve of the *hijra,* and it has often been associated with Abraha's invasion of 552. But the identification with Abraha's campaign has by no means won universal assent, and the Quranic Year of the Elephant *('ām al-fīl)* must remain an uncertain date. But that it occurred during the reign of Abraha is more than likely, and that it had something to do with his interest in diminishing the authority of the Kaʿba seems no less likely.

Surprisingly in 2009 another inscription concerning Abraha's military initiatives turned up in Bi'r Murayghān.[20] It is undated but must follow the inscription of 552, as it records the removal of ʿAmr from the leadership position into which Abraha had placed him. The new inscription declares a victory of Abraha that re-established his own authority over the Maʿadd and enlarged his territories to the northeast and northwest, so as now to include Yathrib. This campaign at some date after 552 brought Abraha's realm to its greatest size. It had emerged as a major Christian state between Byzantine Palestine and Persian Iraq. But it was not to endure.

Although Abraha had conspicuously detached his Ethiopian forces from the rulers in Axum, the collapse of the Ethiopian monarchy about this time, as suggested by the drying up of its coinage, must have weakened the Ethiopian presence under Abraha in Arabia. He was succeeded at some time after 560 by two ineffectual and violent sons, one of whom bore, in the Arab tradition, the name of Yaksum—clearly a deformation of Aksum. The radiance of the victories recounted in the Bi'r Murayghān inscriptions gave way to a gloom that seems to have discouraged the Arabs of the peninsula and ultimately to have allowed the Persians to reestablish the links with Arabia that they had formerly created in the age of the Jewish kings.

In the wake of the disastrous administration of Abraha's sons, a certain Sayf ibn dhī Yazan undertook to bring in an external power to expel the Ethiopians. He is said to have undertaken an embassy to the Byzantine emperor and offered Arab submission to his rule in return for driving out the Ethiopians. But the emperor in Constantinople wasted no time in refusing the offer, which, as al-Ṭabarī noted, would have entailed the dispatch of a governor to the region and a wholly new administrative organization.[21] And so Sayf turned, by way of the Naṣrids, to the Persian king Khosroes, who readily agreed to his request and sent a general called Wahrīz (though this may have been his title rather than his name) to lead the necessary military operations and to put the Persians in charge.

What Abraha left behind was a toxic legacy of struggle between the Christians and pagan polytheists, with the confrontation between the Qalīs at Ṣanʿāʾ and the Kaʿba at Mecca symbolizing this struggle. He had boldly and successfully extended his territory into central and western Arabia and thereby incorporated Kinda. He had brought his power close to Mecca. But whether marauding birds deflected him miraculously from this target will always be a mystery.

His regime had spelled the decline of the old capital of the Ḥimyarites at Ẓafār in the mountains below

Mārib and southeast of Ṣan'ā'. It lost its luster in Abraha's reign because he had clearly preferred the two other cities. But recent archaeological work by a team from Heidelberg at Ẓafār has now revealed a haunting relief of a mustachioed, crowned, and clearly Christian king.[22] In addition, sculpture and reliefs from the site suggest more Christian activity in the city than had been suspected before, including the existence of a church.[23] But the excavations do not provide any support for the implausibly detailed account of Christian churches at Ẓafār that figure in the largely fictional narrative that survives concerning an unhistorical saint known as Gregentius.[24]

The power vacuum left behind by the disappearance of the house of Abraha allowed the Persians to take over the region. They brought with them their ancient alliance with Arabian Jews and their patronage of the Naṣrids in al-Ḥīra. They do not appear to have made any effort to import Zoroastrianism into Arabia, but for their purposes this was hardly necessary. They had sufficient support already from the Jewish communities that survived the conquest of Kālēb and from the pagans who maintained polytheist cults in traditional places, which were fewer

Christian king, image from excavation at Zafār, courtesy of Carmen and Paul Yule, Heidelberg.

than before and yet still conspicuous. It was not a good time for Christians. Between the end of Christianity in Arabia in 560 or thereabouts and the canonical birthdate of Muḥammad in about 570, the Persians had a decade to consolidate their influence. Byzantium could no longer look to the enfeebled kingdom in Ethiopia for help in Arabia, and the

Byzantine emperor had prudently reached an accommodation with the Sassanian king. Neither he nor the Persian shah had the slightest reason to imagine that a prophet would soon arise in Mecca who would change the course of world history.

2

ARAB PAGANISM IN LATE ANTIQUITY

FOR NEARLY 200 YEARS, from about 380 until 560, Arabia had incorporated a monotheist state, first Jewish and then Christian, in its southwestern kingdom of Ḥimyar (roughly modern Yemen). For the last 140 years of that period its rulers were Arabs who had converted conspicuously to Judaism. For reasons still unknown, the Ethiopians imported Christianity to Arabia from Axum for only a few years in the late 490s, but soon thereafter Jewish Arab rule was restored until it exploded in the savage persecution of Christians at Najrān. This provoked the Ethiopians to return in 525 and to establish the Christian kingdom that grew and flourished under King Abraha for nearly forty years. It was only after Abraha's death that the Persians assumed control of Arabia, and that was at the invitation of the Arabs themselves.

With Arabia's submission to the authority of Zoroastrian Persians, state-sponsored monotheism in

Arabia came to an end. The Jewish and Christian communities that survived were left without international patrons, but they clearly continued to practice their faith in cities, such as San'ā' or Ẓafār for the Christians, and Ẓafār and Yathrib for the Jews.[1] The long years of Jewish and Christian monotheism as the religion of government naturally contributed to the decline of pagan cults, for which temples became markedly fewer as the sixth century progressed. But the cults that survived remained much as they were before the monotheist centuries. Paganism had traditionally been polytheist, and no less traditionally it was associated with desert tribes.

The Ka'ba in Mecca, to which the tribes still came on pilgrimages, constituted a sacred space *(ḥaram)* that was not only urban but boasted more than a local constituency. Other cities, such as Dūmat al-jandal and Ṭā'if, also had polytheist shrines. But if the Arabic tradition that pre-Islamic idolatry numbered 360 gods is a fantasy, to reduce the number to one, as has been claimed in recent years, with Allāh as the sole god, would be a fantasy of comparable proportion.[2] Polytheism in the late sixth century left enough traces on stone found today to leave no doubt that, however much the monotheist rulers may have weakened idol worship, idols were still both numerous and numinous. Allusions to the worship of these idols was catalogued in detail by Ibn al-Kalbī in a text that only became accessible late in the last century.[3] Although he was writing after the revelations to the Prophet Muḥammad, and his evidence is circumstantial, he seems, in his comparisons with cults outside Arabia (such as those at Palmyra), reasonably well informed.

It is not easy nowadays to use the word "paganism" in discussing religious beliefs, simply because it has no clear meaning. It is usually defined by what it is not, and in the Graeco-Roman Mediterranean context that meant neither Jewish nor Christian. The word "pagan" *(paganus)* evokes a Latin word for a rustic or country person, and it is certainly true that many local cults, such as those that worship trees, springs, and other natural features, would explain such a designation. But in Greek the early Christian word for pagan *(ethnikos)* pointed simply to ethnic or national differences. It was formed from *ethnos* (nation), a word much like *goy* in Hebrew, which meant "nation" in the Bible but later changed to designate any non-Jew, and the Septuagint translation of the Bible into Greek naturally facilitated this change. Greek *ethnikos* was then literally matched by the Latin equivalent *gentilis,* and both eventually came, like *goy*, as well as the English Gentile, to designate non-Jews.[4]

Meanwhile, *ethnikos* in the sense of pagan gave way in later Christian texts to *hellēn* (Greek) because after Constantine the cultivation of classical Greek culture was generally linked to pagan Greek religion—neither Christian nor Jewish. But *hellēn*, although an increasingly common word for paganism in later Greek, never wholly lost its connection with Hellenism, and this could be profoundly embarrassing for a Christian like Gregory of Nazianzus, who had been educated in classical Greek learning.[5] In general, the word "polytheism" is infinitely preferable to paganism because, unlike paganism, it has a precise meaning, which is the worship of many gods.

Surprisingly it took scholars of the modern era a long time to come to the banal realization that pagan cults that were indisputably polytheist often showed a hierarchy of gods, with a supreme god such as Jupiter or Zeus over all. Consequently this realization has inspired a flood of attempts to legitimate something called "pagan monotheism" or even "soft monotheism."[6] But no one familiar with Greek cults could possibly imagine that the pre-Christian Greeks were monotheists, even if in later antiquity various unnamed gods were occasionally perceived as parts *(merē)* of a single god. That is most famously shown in the so-called Tübingen Theosophy, from which one oracle appears on an inscription at Oenoanda in Anatolia.[7] But such thinking arose from the philosophical reflections of later Platonism, and ideas of this kind shared their roots with Christian theology as it spread throughout the Roman Empire. These ideas may have actually been influenced by Platonism, since paganism and Christianity had much more fruitful interaction than is sometimes imagined. It is hardly a secret that many of the Church Fathers, like Gregory of Nazianzus, were steeped in the works of Plato. The recently fashionable attention to pagan monotheism, traces of which can undoubtedly be found, as the Tübingen Theosophy shows, is limited in its application. Paganism that was polytheist did not die, and it goes without saying that there can be no such absurdity as polytheist monotheism, nor even soft monotheism.

The pre-Islamic gods, however many there may have been, had distinctive names, as we know both from inscriptions and from the Qur'ān, quite apart from the later register of Ibn al-Kalbī. The most resonant of those names was Allāh, which, as the whole world knows, ultimately became the name for the single God of Muslim monotheism. But this name and this god had a long pedigree, which goes back at least to the fifth century BC, when Herodotus mentioned a feminine form of the name, Alilat.[8] She emerges in later centuries with her name contracted to Allāt, and she was probably a consort of Allāh. At Palmyra she was worshipped as a part of the pantheon of which Ibn al-Kalbī was well aware, and a marble statue of her, discovered on the site, represented her as an Arab Athena. Greek polytheism regularly nourished Arab polytheism through fruitful similarities of function and appearance. The large-eyed face on a wall painting at Qaryat al-Fāw and a statue of a hermaphrodite at the same site illustrate this cross-fertilization memorably.[9]

Examples could be multiplied. Ares served as a Greek name for the Ethiopian pagan divinity Maḥrem and also for the biblical ʿAr, which surfaced when the Nabataean toponym Rabbathmoba was transformed into Areopolis. The proliferation of pagan angels that is apparent in the Greek world of this time, particularly in Asia Minor with its abundant local paganisms, is echoed in Arabia with angels that had divine powers that may have been connected with traditional gods as messengers. Exactly as the Greek word *angelos,* meaning "messenger," became the word for angel, the Arabic *malak,* formed from an archaic root *la-'a-ka,* meaning "to send," takes on the sense of angel. Representations of Arabian pagan angels, such as the winged Sabaean angel Shams, convey the authority of such beings over the fate of people.[10]

The Arab goddess al-'Uzzā, who was well known to Muḥammad, as a verse of the Qur'ān (53:19–20) proves, had many cults and betyls, notably at Petra, Ramm, and Teima. That same verse names her along with two other pagan goddesses, al-Manāt and Allāt. Although al-'Uzzā could be assimilated to the Greek Aphrodite, she was as different from Allāt as Aphrodite was from Athena. Allāt's name is a feminine form of Allāh, but she was obviously not the same as Athena, whose iconography represented her at Palmyra, nor was she a female instantiation of Allāh, any more than Zeus's consort Hera was a female Zeus. Neither was she a daughter of Allāh, as has recently been suggested. There are no daughters of Allāh mentioned in the Qur'ān, although daughters are found in contemporary inscriptions. They existed as goddesses in their own right in Palmyra and Arabia, and one of them even had an angel of her own.[11]

In the Quranic verse that mentions the three goddesses Muḥammad mockingly asks his pagan opponents whether they have actually seen them, which would suggest that those opponents certainly knew what the goddesses looked like because they had seen images of them. That was more than he could claim for his own Lord, of whom, by his own admission, he had seen only signs. The diversity of the pre-Islamic gods was reflected in their images both in relief and in sculpture, and the epigraphy shows the pantheon to have been as thoroughly polytheist as the images and epigraphy of the Greek gods. In fact, the third of the goddesses invoked by Muḥammad, al-Manāt, appears in five inscriptions from Madā'in Ṣāliḥ, which was the ancient Hegra not far from Medina, and ibn al-Kalbī appropriately reports that her cult was conspicuous between Mecca and Medina.[12] The goddesses named by Muḥammad in addressing his pagan opponents make it plain that he knew about the traditional cults as reflections of polytheism. They could not conceivably have been incorporated in some kind of monotheist conceptual framework.

But this does not preclude, after two centuries of Jewish and Christian rule in the peninsula, the emergence of diverse forms of pagan Arab monotheism in addition to the monotheism of Muḥammad. In fact, several prophets arose to compete with Muḥammad in proclaiming a single god, and despite the lack of contemporary documentation for these prophets, it is most unlikely that they were all fabricated by writers after Muḥammad's death, and it will be necessary to return to them in subsequent chapters. The most famous and aggressive of the monotheist prophets who are recorded in the Arab tradition is Musaylima. His sphere of influence seemed to have been largely confined to Yamāma in central Arabia.[13] He is alleged to have had his own unique god called Rahmān, his own revelations, and his own Qur'ān. He is reported ultimately to have made contact with Muḥammad and then to have continued his mission until he was finally eliminated in the Wars of Apostasy *(ridda)* under the first caliph, Abū Bakr.

It is therefore important to remember that Muḥammad was not the only monotheist prophet to emerge in late sixth-century Arabia, nor was Musaylima the only other one, according to Arab tradition. It appears that out of the ferment of Jewish and Christian communities, as well as the ever-widening circulation of Neoplatonic theology in Hellenized parts of the Near East, particularly to the north in Syrian Apamea, concepts of monotheism were perfectly compatible with a single god who was not the god of the Jews or Christians.[14] But this is by no means the same as postulating that all pagans had become monotheist. Traditional paganism left its traces all over the Arab world of late antiquity, and these show that polytheism, though diminished, had an undoubtedly robust activity after the Persians assumed control in Arabia. Muḥammad certainly had to deal with polytheists.

The word that Muḥammad used for those pagans, *mushrikūn,* has long been understood to imply polytheism. A *mushrik* "shared" *(sharika)* or "associated" the objects of his worship, and it would be hard for anyone who knows about other forms of polytheism, above all in the Greek and Roman contexts, to see this as anything other than the recognition of multiple divinities. These divinities naturally had different functions, but none eclipsed another. The Qur'ān clearly distinguishes the *mushrikūn* from both Jews and Christians, who represented at the time the most prominent monotheist faiths. Significantly the Qur'ān also distinguishes the *mushrikūn* from two clearly specified groups of monotheists, who were neither Jews nor Christians and must therefore be presumed pagans of some kind. The words *ṣabī* and *ḥanīf* are used to describe an Arab who was not a Jew, not a Christian, and not a *mushrik.*

The precise meaning of *ṣabī* in the Qur'ān is not certain, but it evidently evoked a monotheist, and there is good reason to think that this category of pagan monotheism reappeared in Neoplatonist theology that turned up surprisingly after many centuries in Ḥarrān. It was there that the tenth-century Muslim historian Mas'ūdī discovered a thriving community of Arab Platonists, with a quotation from their master on the lintel of one of their meeting places.[15] Although a Quranic *ṣabī* need not have been the same as a late antique Neoplatonist, this would be by no means out of the question. Julian the Apostate had long before demonstrated that Neoplatonism, by way of Iamblichus, had turned into a quasi-religion, and subsequent philosophy, as developed by the later Neoplatonists, moved in the same direction through the teaching and thought of Proclus and others. It may well have been that the spiritual ancestors of the "Sabians" of the Ḥarrān were pagan monotheists active in Arabia in the late sixth century.

If we consider a *ḥanīf* as a pagan who was not polytheist, we are on somewhat firmer ground. A famous reference to Abraham in the third sura of the Qur'ān (verse 67) explicitly tells us what Abraham was not, and also what he was: "Abraham was neither a Jew nor a Christian, but he was *ḥanīfan musliman,* and he was not one of the *mushrikūn.*" So he was not a Jew, a Christian, or a polytheist, but a *ḥanīf* who had found his way to the truth about God. The word *muslim* in this text antedates its use as an adjective for an adherent of Islam, but it suggests an early perception of the truth inherent in Muḥammad's faith. Uri Rubin and others have noticed that *ḥanīf* is a word that was used both for the Prophet's Believers and for those who opposed him, and its Syriac cognate *ḥanpā* is the word for "apostate."[16] The use of this term with *muslim* in the third sura implies the positive sense of this word, and Aziz al-Azmeh is quite right to emphasize that it is important to bear in mind that the triliteral root of *ḥanīf* means "to turn aside" or "to diverge."[17] If one turns aside to the good and true, one becomes a *ḥanīf* like Abraham or the supporters of Muḥammad, but if one turns aside to what is false, one becomes an apostate and an enemy. Abraham, whose father had reportedly been a polytheist pagan, became the progenitor of the Jews and the Arabs, according to biblical tradition, through unions with his wife Sara and his servant Hagar, and in doing so he "turned aside" from worshipping many gods to the worship of the one true God.

Abraham was also credited with the creation of the Kaʿba at Mecca, but since this was a shrine for pagan gods in the historical period down to Muḥammad we must assume that Abraham's original purpose was subverted, or at least that the tradition presupposed that it was. The Quranic Abraham was explicitly not a *mushrik,* and if Abraham was a pagan monotheist this necessarily indicates that a *mushrik* was a pagan polytheist. Hence we must understand the Quranic *mushrikūn* as polytheists. Quite apart from Arabian gods worshipped at Dūmat al-jandal, Ramm, Teima, Madā'in Ṣāliḥ, and Mecca, the references in the Qur'ān to pagan angels reinforce the case for polytheism at the end of the sixth century. The pagan opponents of the Prophet wondered why, if Muḥammad was communicating a divine revelation, an angel *(malak)* or angels *(malā'ik)* would not have appeared to intercede with them to announce the divine source of his message.[18]

This was not a frivolous objection, because late antique paganism, both in Arabia and in the outside Hellenic world, had many angels, some of whom had been sent by a god. After all, the classical Greek word *angelos* originally meant "messenger," and in Greek mythology messengers such as Hermes or Iris never became angels. The word *angelos* was taken over by the translators of the Septuagint to render the biblical *mal'ak,* and it was this usage that gradually led to the disappearance of *angelos* in the original sense of messenger. It was replaced in Christian Greek by *apostolos,* whereas in the sense of angel it was absorbed into Latin simply as *angelus.* In classical and modern Arabic an angel is *malak,* without the alif, although that may once have been there, to judge from a rare but attested Arabic verb, *la-'a-ka,* to send. Some of those pagan angels could even be gods in their own right, just as the daughters of Allāh could be goddesses. In Greek inscriptions from the Near East even Zeus himself can be an angel.[19]

It is therefore important that Muḥammad saw himself as a Messenger *(rasūl),* bringing God's word, but at no time did he ever describe himself as an angel *(malak).* He explicitly denied that he was one.[20] That is presumably why his enemies pressed him on the point that an angel had not been sent to them to confirm that his message had a divine source. The "noble messenger" of Sura 81 who is influential with the holder of the divine throne is presumably precisely that, a messenger and not an angel. Muḥammad himself was a noble messenger. We need now to accept, at least until someone can disprove it, the proposition that the distinction in Arabic between *rasūl* and *malak* was never blurred in Quranic usage. The very separation of the two terms and concepts provides a window into the different mentalities of Muḥammad's Believers and the Arab polytheists.

3

LATE ANTIQUE MECCA

MUSLIM TRADITION REPORTS that Muḥammad's tribe, the Quraysh, arrived in Mecca out of the Banu Kināna only a century or so before his birth. How the tribe of the Quraysh found its way there or why they settled in such a place is unknown.[1] The site lay in a valley that endured an inhospitable climate in hot weather, but it had at least the advantage of security that nature provided with a formidable chain of mountains that stretched southward from the Jordanian border in the north along the western side of the Ḥijāz. These were the *jibāl al-sirawāt* (or *al-sirat*) that extended along the eastern coastline of the Gulf of 'Aqaba and Red Sea, where anchorages were few. Among these were Yanbu' and, south of it, Jidda, near which a gap in the mountains afforded Mecca an opening in the great rocky barrier. The mountainous chain continued southward from there, at a somewhat higher elevation, through the region of 'Asīr along the coast and down into western Yemen.

It is evident that geography had predetermined that trade, travel, and military expeditions coming up from the south would reach Mecca through the interior of the western Arabian peninsula. From Mecca the journey northward went directly into Medina and from there to ʿal-ʿUlā, Ḥijr (Hegra, Madāʾin Ṣāliḥ), and Tabūk. The caravan traffic in perfumes and spices from the vicinity of Aden is normally assumed to have gone northward to the city of Najrān and then to have swung westward over toward Bīsha to avoid the inhospitable lava fields that lay above Najrān. Mecca was a natural destination in this northward movement, and pilgrims and traders would easily have found Ukāz and Ṭāʾif appropriate way stations to the city because of their regular cycle of fairs.[2]

Because nature had ensured that Mecca needed no walls, it was accessible from the interior of Arabia. It resembled Petra in its mountainous isolation from the adjacent peoples and lines of communication, at the same time as sitting alongside the major north-south line of communication. It also resembled Petra in its sanctity, preserving the black cubic shrine *(ḥaram)* of at least one important local god in the pagan pantheon. No one can say when the bizarre basalt cube called the Kaʿba was built at Mecca, but its existence was traditionally believed to go back as far as Abraham. Nor can anyone say whether Hubal was the god first worshipped there. But by the time of Muḥammad it is clear from the Qur'ān that Allāh was already a major, and perhaps even the principal, god of the town. But whether he shared his cult with Hubal, a god that the Arabs associated with the Ka'ba, remains a mystery to this day.[3]

Such hospitality to pagan divinities is again comparable to Petra, where an underground shrine, recently excavated beneath the Khazneh, commemorates an ancient cult of a local deity, who was probably Dushāra, the deity of the Sharā escarpment. But we know that he was by no means alone. An inscribed stele depicting haunting eyes, nose, and mouth reveals that the populace of Petra also revered the goddess al-'Uzza, a goddess associated particularly with Nakhla in Arabia.[4] Another dedication in Petra was made to Atargatis.[5]

Accordingly, the settlement of Mecca by the Quraysh, whenever it may have occurred during the period of just a few generations before the Prophet, reflected both the ancient sacrality of the space and the physical security that its location provided. The gods of the place, including Hubal and Allāh above all, are known to have flourished alongside other divinities, such as Manāf, Isāf, and Nā'ila, who kept company with those famous goddesses who are mentioned in the Qur'ān—Manāt, al-'Uzza, and Allāt.[6] Although it is generally agreed by now that Mecca was not founded on a pre-existing caravan route, any more than Petra was, it was obviously settled as a secure and holy place that was not far removed from the caravan route. It is twice called the "Mother of Cities" *(umm al-qurā)* in the Qur'ān.[7] The movement of traders and goods to the south and east of Mecca was apparent both from the great fair at 'Ukāz and the temples not far distant in al-Ṭā'if and Tabāla. More portentous for the future was the great oasis city known in the sixth century as Yathrib, which lay several hundred kilometers to the north. This was later to become the Medina of the Muslims, to which Muḥammad would make his *hijra* when he departed, along with his Believers, from Mecca.

The conventional modern vision of Mecca as a mercantile city, which was introduced over a century ago by the Belgian scholar Henri Lammens, has understandably come under attack in recent decades for its exaggerated representation of the city's commercial activity.[8] But the countervailing wholesale demolition of the former mercantile image of the city, as launched by Patricia Crone nearly three decades ago, has become increasingly untenable and was vigorously repudiated at the time, on points of Arabic, by Robert Serjeant.[9] Even Crone, who could bring herself to acknowledge only Meccan trade in hides and leather, eventually came to realize that this trade in mundane but important materials, which she had acknowledged at the same time as disparaging it for being ludicrously modest, was in fact far more substantial than she had imagined.[10]

It is true that many perfumes and spices from southern Arabia tended by this late date to make their way into the Graeco-Roman world by shipping through the Red Sea up into the Gulf of ʿAqaba, with a brief overland transit to the Mediterranean or an onward journey northward by caravan. Even this pattern would not preclude the movement of perfumes and spices to be sold at the great fairs in Arabia and consumed by those who lived along the route through the Ḥijāz. In addition, pre-Islamic Mecca engaged in trade with Ethiopia, presumably on Ethiopian ships. Although there is no way of judging the extent of any commerce with Axum, the presence of Meccans in that city during the time of Muḥammad proves that the two cities were in contact.[11] The mercantile reputation of Mecca under the Quraysh was certainly no mirage, and if we have not returned precisely to the image promulgated by Montgomery Watt, against whose vision Crone was reacting, we are no longer far removed from it.[12]

Crone had even denied that Mecca was known at all before the seventh century, but to argue for this she was obliged to ignore the apparent presence of this site in the second-century register of the geographer Ptolemy.[13] A place called Makoraba is listed more or less together with places where we should expect Mecca to be, though longitudes are notoriously treacherous in Ptolemy. But its coordinates approximate the actual location of the town. In fact it lies conspicuously to the south of another place that Ptolemy calls Lathrippa, which is undoubtedly the oasis at Yathrib. Although it may not be immediately obvious that Makoraba is a Greek deformation of the name of Mecca (or Makka, as it is in Arabic), Ptolemy's location of Makoraba makes it highly likely that the first syllable does indeed incorporate the name Makka. If so, the second half of Ptolemy's name would reproduce the Aramaic *rabb* (great), implying preeminence, and it could, like other Aramaic borrowings in Arabia, have easily seeped into the local language through the Jews we know to have been in Yathrib and elsewhere.

It is worth comparing the ancient Rabbat-Moab in Transjordan, which was the city that the Romans knew as Areopolis. More pertinently, the name of Mecca in Arabic, Makka, is regularly followed by the adjective *mukarram* ("noble"). Ptolemy's Makoraba would therefore seem not only to preserve the ancient nomenclature and coordinates of Mecca, but even a correlative, reverential adjective, which presumably reflected the existence of the Ka'ba. This cubic shrine had famously made Mecca both a sacred place and a destination for pagan pilgrims. So with Ptolemy it is likely that we have a record of the city that antedates by some four centuries the alleged settlement of the Quraysh at Mecca. It is impossible to know who was there in Ptolemy's day, but, like most local shrines in antiquity, it seems to have been recognized as a holy place from time immemorial.

Some historians have explored a different interpretation of Makoraba by invoking the Sabaic and Ethiopic *mkrb/makwrab,* meaning a temple or place of association (it can also mean a synagogue), but this seems a less compelling reading of Ptolemy's name than an actual transmission of the name of Mecca

(Makka) together with an aggrandizing adjective that matches the adjective that is found in Arabic.[14] The Ka'ba was hardly a temple or a place of assembly, but rather a pilgrimage site. In fact by the late fourth century, when the historian Ammianus Marcellinus had occasion to register the cities of western Arabia, he named seven places, one of which was oddly Dioscorides, which is the classical name for the island of Socotra off the southern coast. But other sites known to Ammianus included the cities of Naskos and Nagara (Najrān), both named in Ptolemy.[15] Of the notable *civitates* that Marcellinus names, most can be identified, notably Maephe, which is Mepha in Ptolemy, and Taphra, which is Sapphara in Ptolemy.

But a puzzling outlier among Ammianus's Arabian *civitates* is Geapolis or, in a variant reading, Hierapolis. If this variant has any authority, this city looks very much like the "holy city" *(hiera polis)* of Mecca.[16] It would therefore be reasonable to interpret these scraps in Ammianus and Ptolemy as confirming what we would naturally infer in any case, that a pagan shrine or *ḥaram* that included a conspicuous black cube as a sacred relic would have been known as a holy city. It seems from the tradition of Abraha's construction of his sumptuous church of al-Qalīs, not to mention his march to the north with the famous elephant, that he was well aware of Mecca's reputation, and his aborted march against the shrine may be seen as commemorating not only his militant zeal but the prestige of Mecca itself at that time. The temples of which we hear at Dūmat al-Jandal or at al-Ṭā'īf clearly lacked comparable prestige. Not even the burgeoning discipline of "Quranic archaeology," which Mikhail Piotrovsky has recently hailed as the Islamicists' answer to biblical archaeology, has so far been able to reveal any great temples.[17]

Fortunately the Qur'ān itself provides a well-known clue to the nature of the trading activity of late antique Mecca. It does so in Sura 106, entitled "Quraysh." In the canonical text this sura immediately follows the sura of the Elephant *(al-fīl)*, which has often been taken to be an allusion to Abraha's aborted march on Mecca. It explicitly mentions Qurashi expeditions in winter and summer that were protected by a guarantee of safe passage *(īlāf)*. These expeditions cohere perfectly with historical reports of journeys each year to Yemen and to Syria.[18] Although the goods conveyed to these regions may well have been hides, leathers, and textiles, they could also have included wine from the Ṭā'īf region, as Mikhail Bukharin has recently suggested, perhaps destined for transfer to India.[19] In returning to Mecca from these seasonal expeditions, the traders could have brought spices, perfumes, aloe, and balsam from southern Arabia, and from Syria they could have brought much-needed grain.

As Abraha had recognized, the fame and prosperity of Mecca depended principally upon the pilgrims who visited its shrine and its sacred space *(ḥaram)*. Qurashi control of the pilgrimages depended upon the successful but fragile union of various tribal communities in the region, such as the Kināna and the Ghatafān. When the future Prophet Muḥammad came into the world in or about the year 570 he and the Quraysh, to which he belonged, inherited a community of tribal equanimity that allowed, at least for a time, ample space for the revelations he was to claim forty years later he received from the angel Gabriel (Jibrīl). But it is important to remember that his assumption of the mantle of a prophet was not all that exceptional in a holy city such as Mecca, particularly in a part of central Arabia that conspicuously nourished prophecy that could be both inspiring and divisive at the same time. Among Arabs of the Arabian peninsula who had found themselves living among Jews and Christians in territory that had been ruled by a succession of Jewish kings in Ḥimyar, and after that by Christian Ethiopian kings, the ingredients for nurturing seers and prophets were everywhere. The Jewish population of Yathrib had been there for centuries and enjoyed prominence and prestige. Until the arrival of the Persian overlords after Abraha and his sons, Christians were well known to the pagan Arabs, and what those Arabs borrowed from Jews or Christians could readily be supplemented from the Zoroastrianism of the Persians themselves, who showed themselves exceptionally astute in cohabiting with Christians.[20]

There can be little doubt that when Muḥammad was reaching maturity, the cults in central and southwestern Arabia under Persian domination were embedded in a thick context that went back at least as far as the late fourth century, and were an amalgam that was part Jewish, part Christian, and part polytheist. This was fertile ground for a charismatic prophet like Muḥammad, but also for comparably charismatic figures in the Arabian hinterland not far away from Mecca. The efflorescence of prophets and prophecy in Persian Arabia when Muḥammad began to receive his revelations from Gabriel is well known to the Arabic tradition. Although no contemporary documentation exists for these rival charismatics, the richness and diversity of subsequent testimony for them in the Arabic tradition strongly suggests that even when Muḥammad was still at Mecca Arabs were receptive to visionaries who were very much like him. In short, he was not unique in his own time and had to assert his claim as the unique messenger to be bringing the word of Allāh to the Arabs. Whether he was the first of his generation to do this or, as seems much more probable, one among many in the same generation will never be known. But the fact is that he was by no means alone in proclaiming revelations that were both cognizant of Jewish and Christian monotheism and arose in a pagan context.[21] His were the revelations that ultimately prevailed.

The most famous of those rival prophets, according to the Arabic tradition, was Musaylima from the banu Ḥanīfa in al-Yamāma in central Arabia to the east of Mecca.[22] He was more than a soothsayer *(kāhin)* and had been receiving revelations from Gabriel already before Muḥammad left Mecca for Medina in 622. He could thus present himself as a prophet *(nabī)* whose verses in rhymed prose *(sajʿ)* constituted an independent Qur'ān, of which thirty-three verses still survive. Although they are different from verses in the canonical Qur'ān, they show clear similarities. At about the same time as Musaylima, or perhaps a little later, another prophet arose in Arabia, in Yemen between Ṭā'if and Aden. This was Aswad al-ʿansī, who also received revelations and compiled his own Qur'ān. Both Musaylima and Aswad were remembered subsequently as part of the struggles of the first caliph after Muḥammad's death, Abū Bakr, to eliminate them and their followers as threats to the supremacy of the Islamic Believers. But it seems certain that they were well established in their prophetic roles before the so-called *ridda*, which represented the reaction against Islam after Muḥammad's death in what is sometimes called inappropriately the "Wars of Apostasy." It is important to remember that these opponents of Islam were largely rival prophets and in no way apostates, and their prophecies antedated the *ridda*.

Musaylima evidently posed the greatest challenge to Muḥammad, whose supporters dispatched missions to al-Yamāma to promote Islam. It seems that Musaylima, whose very name is a diminutive form of Maslama, bore a name that was formed from the same verbal root as Muslim and Islam. It unmistakably implies a direct confrontation with the Prophet in Mecca and subsequently in Medina. The two men are said actually to have met in Medina. It seems clear that Musaylima never denied the prophetic role of Muḥammad, but he believed that the two of them should share their messages, and that they should divide their responsibilities between Medina and al-

Yamāma. The Arabs preserved the text of a famous letter in which Musaylima proposed this division to Muḥammad. Of course, like every other document from this early period, the authenticity of Musaylima's letter cannot be confirmed, but it would be reasonable to assume that it mirrors some kind of diplomatic contact or negotiation between the two prophets at a date after the *hijra* in 622 and before Muḥammad's death in 632.

The text of this letter, which exists in slightly different versions, shows Musaylima presenting himself as another messenger, who is the equal of Muḥammad: "From Musaylima the messenger of God to Muḥammad the messenger of God. Peace be upon you hereafter. Indeed, I have been made partner with you in in authority. To us belongs half of the land and to the Quraysh the other half, but the Quraysh are the people who transgress."[23] God is here named Allāh, as generally in the canonical Qur'ān, but we are told that Musaylima had at least at one time himself adopted the name al-Raḥmān, "the merciful," as the divine name, thereby appropriating a Sabaean word that had entered the Arabian vocabulary during the reigns of the Jewish Arab kings of Ḥimyar. Muḥammad's Qur'ān (17.210) clearly recognized al-Raḥmān as an alternate name for Allāh, and Musaylima's use of Allāh in the received version of his letter seems to imply a time in which God's name had now become fixed. There was even an Arabic tradition that at one stage in his career Musaylima was himself called Raḥmān, although there is no trace of this in the document in which he proposed dividing his authority with Muḥammad.

The Prophet's reply to the suggestion that he share his prophetic mission is a withering rejection of Musaylima's invitation. It begins significantly with the canonical Islamic *bismillah,* "In the name of God the merciful *(raḥmān)* and compassionate," and it states that Muḥammad "the messenger *(rasūl)* of God" is replying to Musaylima, who is now not another messenger but "the arch liar *(al-kadhdhāb).*" Muḥammad picks up the reference to peace in Musaylima's letter by saying, "Peace hereafter be upon those who follow guidance. The land belongs to God. He lets whom He will of His creatures inherit it and the result is to the pious." This reply combines a pointed response to Musaylima's letter, through its use of "messenger" only for the Prophet himself, through its reformulation of the peace clause, and through its rejection of the proposal about the land. All this is introduced by the unmistakably Islamic *bismillah.* The whole text sounds very much like Muḥammad at Medina and probably not long before his death. But the exchange, to the extent that it incorporates authentic notions and phrases, reveals much about the spiritual world of Arabia and its competing prophets in the early seventh century. Islam would eventually emerge triumphant amid the noisy claimants to prophecy and religious leadership in the region.

4

ETHIOPIA AND ARABIA

Ethiopian intervention in the Arabian peninsula from the second to the sixth centuries had left unmistakable traces of the ambitions of the *negus* in Axum to control the territory that lay immediately across the Red Sea from his kingdom. The conquests that were proudly proclaimed in the long inscription on a marble throne, which is now lost, at the port of Axum in Adulis (modern Zula) illustrated the expansionist policies of an unnamed ruler, who was probably Sembrouthes, or perhaps Gadarat, in the early third century. These conquests served as a basis for later irredentist expeditions to recover land that had once been held in Arabia.[1] The placement of this throne at Adulis alongside an earlier inscription of Hellenistic date suggests that Axumite campaigns overseas in the Ptolemaic period had inspired the campaigns in Arabia under the Roman Empire. Ethiopian inscriptions show that the *negus* in Axum continued to register Arabian territories in his royal titulature even when Ethiopians no longer actually occupied them. The symbiosis of Arabia and Ethiopia is mirrored in the script for the language, Ge'ez, that was used at Axum. It was borrowed closely from the Sabaic script of South Arabia, and Axumite inscriptions conveyed their message in both languages and both scripts. Ethiopians continued to use Greek as well, which reinforced their place in the greater Byzantine Empire. The anonymous author of the *Periplus of the Red Sea* had already remarked on their facility in Greek during the first century.[2]

By an astonishing coincidence the Arabs of Ḥimyar converted to Judaism in the late fourth century at about the same time as the monarchy at Axum adopted Christianity. The first Christian *negus,* Aizanas, left behind grandiose inscriptions at Axum that served as a constant, visible reminder not only of his religion but of the territories he claimed to rule. His successors could draw inspiration not only from his piety but from his shameless arrogation of titles to authority in southwestern Arabia, where the Ethiopians had ruled in the previous century, even though they no longer did. This meant that just as the Arab converts to Judaism were becoming increasingly intolerant of the Christian communities in their midst, the Ethiopian Christians were becoming increasingly zealous in promoting their new faith along with recovering their lost domination in the peninsula.

Over the course of the late fifth and early sixth centuries the Jews in Arabia launched their notorious persecutions of Christian communities. The most brutal of these occurred at Najrān in 523, and it providentially provided the Ethiopian Christians with a good reason to renew their irredentist claim to Arabia. They joined forces with the Christian emperors in Byzantium to wipe out the Jewish government in Arabia, without regard for the doctrinal differences that separated Chalcedonian Byzantium from non-Chalcedonian Axum. This happened in 525, after which southwestern and central Arabia soon devolved into a kingdom ruled by an Ethiopian Christian general, Abraha, whose efforts to extend and strengthen his authority in the peninsula went so far, as we have already seen, as to encompass an abortive attempt to take Mecca. That sacred city had already assumed an aggressive role in opposing Abraha's Christian church at San'a' and thereby asserted its prominence as a pilgrimage site for Arab pagans.[3]

When Muḥammad was born, in the vicinity of 570, the Sassanian Persians had been ruling for a decade or more the Arabian territory that Abraha had governed as a Christian kingdom. During this time of

Stele of Aezanas at Axum. Greek text with Ge'ez text in Ethiopic and Sabaic scripts, *Recueil des inscriptions de l'Éthiopie* I, 185 bis and 270 bis, courtesy of Finbarr Barry Flood.

transition, which remains today the most obscure and poorly documented period in the history of late antique Arabia, the Christian populations were marginalized, even as Persia's sympathy for the Jews grew. This sympathy was an inheritance from Persian support of the old Jewish kingdom of Ḥimyar earlier in the century, and it was naturally rooted in in the conflict with Christian Byzantium. Jewish communities, conspicuously those in Yathrib, had reason to look favorably upon the new regime in the peninsula. We have seen that Arab pagans could look with equanimity upon their Persian overlords, because they were never active in promoting Zoroastrianism and probably found the diversity of Arab polytheism useful in preventing any kind of unified resistance. The tribes, clans, and gods of Arabia at this time worked to the advantage of external powers. It was precisely this diversity and disunity that would be a threat to Muḥammad when he first began to receive his revelations from Gabriel and would ultimately be resolved only as the Islamic movement gathered strength.

The Ethiopian kingdom on the other side of the Red Sea in the early years of Muḥammad always had the potential to alter or even to disrupt the stability, fragile at best, in Arabian affairs of the late sixth century. Yet with the end of the Christian kingdom in Arabia no one could predict what impact the Christian *negus* in Axum might have upon the unstable political and religious patterns in Arabia under Persian domination. Ethiopia had intervened across the Red Sea often enough in the past to leave no doubt of its importance in the greater Byzantine world. By the time of Muḥammad it was a sleeping giant that awaited yet another call to life.

The revelations that Gabriel brought to Muḥammad came in Mecca. He belonged to the founding tribe of the Quraysh as a member of the clan of Hāshim, and his paternal uncle, Abū Ṭālib, who raised him, provided him with local support. He married an older and wealthy woman, Khadīja, who was engaged in commerce and secured his standing in the city. But the revelations that began about 610 caused increasing problems for Muḥammad with the Quraysh and the Hāshim in particular. He could of course count upon the support of his wife, but both she and Abū Ṭālib died, leaving him exposed to jealousy and fear from his tribesmen. Although the change in Muḥammad's position has sometimes been imagined to have given rise to factional disputes among the early Believers, there are no grounds for such a conjecture.

But trouble arose from the non-Believers. Those of Muḥammad's followers who now accepted him as the Messenger of God increasingly made his compatriots mistrustful of his strident advocacy of monotheism in a city famous for its *ḥaram* of polytheism. The quarrels with his opponents in Mecca left traces in the Qur'ān, along with the names of some of the divinities he repudiated. A Muslim tradition suggests that he even tried to assuage his enemies by acknowledging the possibility of intercession with God through three pagan goddesses—Allāt, al-ʻUzzā, and al-Manāt. It was this tradition that spawned the now notorious story of the so-called Satanic verses that Satan himself was alleged to have induced the Prophet to include in his Qur'ān. Those verses, which supposedly reveal a short-lived concession from Muḥammad to his antagonists, do not actually appear in the canonical text of the Qur'ān, but traces of them were believed to have survived in the explicit references to the three goddesses in the present Quranic text of the sura of the Star *(al-Najm)*.[4]

The crisis that Muḥammad and his followers had with their opponents in Mecca was the spark that ignited the return of Ethiopia into Arabian affairs, but this time without so much as the slightest direct intervention in the peninsula. Instead of Ethiopians sailing across the Red Sea to invade Arabia, as formerly, it was the Arabs themselves who made the reverse journey to Ethiopia. Because trade with Axum had been a part of the mercantile economy of Mecca, it was presumably on Ethiopian commercial vessels that some of the early Believers, confronting opposition at home, opted to abandon their city to take refuge with the *negus*. As a Christian, this ruler had certainly not espoused the doctrines of nascent Islam, if indeed he knew about them, but he evidently enjoyed a reputation for integrity and piety that was attractive to the newly inspired Arab monotheists in Mecca.

Hence in about 615 a group of Muḥammad's Believers emigrated to Axum in what is sometimes called the first emigration, or *hijra*, an uncanny anticipation of the great *hijra* about seven years later to Medina. In view of the timing of this *hijra*, it is not impossible that the unease of the emigrants may have been exacerbated by news of the Persian capture of Jerusalem the year before, a momentous event that will occupy Chapter 5. It is impossible to be absolutely sure of the chronology, but it is very likely that once news of Persian complicity with the Jews in overthrowing an emblematic Christian city had reached Arabia, the court of the *negus* in Ethiopia might have seemed an increasingly safe place to be. Both hostility in Mecca and a Persian alliance with the Jews would have given the Believers ample reason to flee.[5]

It seems clear from a complex Muslim tradition of stories about the emigrants, who were called "those who made the *hijra*" *(muhājirūn),* that they were hospitably received at Axum and remained there for a considerable number of years despite delegations from the Quraysh who appealed to the *negus* to send them back.[6] A surprising supplement that was added to the story of the first *hijra* is a report that a second one to Axum soon followed the first. Little can be said about this with any confidence, but al-Balādhurī explicitly mentions a second emigration, and it appears that the numbers of refugees were larger than in the first wave.[7] The Arabic tradition is exceptionally rich in accounts of the response of the Ethiopian monarch to his Meccan guests. He is reported to have wept after having hearing recitations from the Qur'ān. When the *negus* died, Muḥammad is said to have performed the ritual prayer, or *ṣalāt,* for him.[8]

It is generally agreed that the *negus* who received the Meccan refugees in Axum in about 615 was in all probability the last Ethiopian ruler to have issued coins.[9] This is a contemporary of Muḥammad who seems to have taken the name Armaḥ and may possibly be the same as Aṣḥam ibn Abjar, a benevolent monarch who is even credited with contributing materials to Muḥummad for rebuilding the Ka'ba. Armaḥ is the name that appears on the bronze and silver coins with which Ethiopian issues come to an end. The silver coins of that issue include an unparalleled image on the reverse, with two pairs of columns supporting an arch with a Greek cross superimposed on it. Separate elongated crosses rise up from the tops of each pair of columns. Within the columns is an inverted triangle with a circle below it. Stuart Munro-Hay saw this as a representation of an ecclesiastical edifice, and it would be hard to disagree with him. His speculation that the edifice in question was none other than the Holy Sepulchre in Jerusalem is attractive in view of the appearance of the church portals that can still be seen today.[10]

If the emigrants from Mecca arrived in Axum soon after the Persian capture of Jerusalem, those last strange coins of the *negus* might reflect news of this event, which proved momentous for Christians throughout the greater Byzantine world. The complex Arabic tradition about the Meccans in Christian Ethiopia is well illustrated in the Quranic acknowledgment that Allāh was able to create Jesus from the Virgin Mary. It seems likely that the *negus* was aware that the revelations to Muḥammad included recognition of the virgin birth and the mission of Jesus, and he is reported to have been so moved by hearing the Prophet's words that in some traditions he accepts that Muḥammad is the messenger of God and even converts secretly to Islam.[11] All of this obviously lies beyond any historical analysis, but it suggests some measure of sympathy between the Muslim Believers and the Ethiopian Christians. The crisis that had just unfolded in Jerusalem may have encouraged some kind of mutual support between these two "Peoples of the Book."

An explicit address to Christians as fellow People of the Book occurs in verse 171 of the fourth sura of the Qur'ān, and this may again reflect the interaction between Mecca and Axum at the time of the first *hijra*. It famously takes up the problem of the Trinity, which would naturally concern any adherents of a new monotheism: "O People of the Book, do not exaggerate in your religion or say anything about Allāh except the truth. The Messiah, Jesus, the son of Mary, was only a messenger of Allāh, and His Word is what He bestowed upon Mary and His Spirit [*rūḥ*, breath]. So believe in Allāh and His messengers. Do not say, 'Three.' Stop. It is better for you. Allāh is but one God. He is far above having a son."

In 628, after Muḥammad's return to Mecca from Medina, he is reported to have sent letters to the leaders of the world around him, to encourage them to embrace Islam and accept his role as the Messenger of God. Allegedly, he wrote to the emperor Heraclius in Constantinople, to the Persian shah Khosroes in Baghdad, to the Muqawqis (perhaps the patriarch) in Alexandria, to al-Ḥārith ibn ʿAbd Kulāl in Ḥimyarite Arabia, and, perhaps most significantly in view of the first *hijra* to Ethiopia, to the reigning *negus,* who would have been Armaḥ, the last attested ruler of that period and the host of the *muhājirūn.* Understandably the authenticity of every one of the Prophet's letters to world rulers has been questioned, although a manuscript of the one to Ḥārith exists in the Sabaic musnad script.[12] This would certainly suggest a very early copy. The letter to Khosroes (Kisra) has found some advocates. The letter to the *negus* explicitly alludes to the Qur'ān on Mary and the virgin birth, as do some reports of Muslim contacts with him.[13] But Muslim tradition is divided about his reception of the letter—telling that the *negus* both rejected the letter by tearing it up and accepted its invitation to convert by swearing allegiance to Muḥammad and espousing Islam.

Obviously it is impossible to extract any reliable information from Muḥammad's letter to the *negus* any more than to the other rulers. But it can stand as a part of a dossier that reflects continuing interest on the part of the first Believers in securing the support of Ethiopian Christians. This dossier begins before Muḥammad's own famous *hijra* to Medina in 622 and probably extends well beyond that. The Quranic echoes are unmistakable.

Muḥammad's message to the *negus* is said to have gone as follows: "In the name of Allāh the Merciful and the Compassionate: From Muḥammad the prophet of Islam to the negus, the king of Ethiopia: peace be upon you. I thank Allāh for you—there is no Allāh but Him—who are the holy king—peace, believer, protector. I witness that Jesus, the son of Mary, is God's Spirit and is His Word. The Word He presented to the good chaste virgin Mary, and from this Word she bore Jesus. Allāh made him from His Spirit [*rūḥ*, breath] just as he made Adam with His hand.[14] I call you and your soldiers to believe in Allāh the Almighty. I have notified and advised you, so accept my advice. Peace upon those who follow the right way."

Ibn Iṣḥaq reported that the *negus* replied to Muḥammad by saying, "I testify that you are the apostle of God, veracious and confirmed, and I have sworn allegiance to you . . . I have become a Muslim . . .

I send you my son." And, in fact, the father of Ibn Iṣḥaq claimed to have seen the son of the *negus* in Mecca, who looked more like an Arab than a black and was big and handsome.[15]

Just about the same time as Muḥammad is alleged to have dispatched his letter to the *negus,* one of the early *muhājirūn* to Axum died. He was Ubaydullāh ibn Jaḥsh. Although precise details of his arrival in Ethiopia and his residence there for more than a decade, apparently between 615 and 627, cannot be recovered, there is no reason to doubt the most remarkable event in his life as an exile. He converted to Christianity, presumably moved by the example of the *negus* as a pious and hospitable ruler. Ubaydullāh was distantly related to the Prophet, and his initial embrace of Islam equipped him with a monotheistic faith that could have found common ground with Christian monotheists. In his *Sīra,* Ibn Isḥāq names Ubaydullāh as one of four notable polytheists in Mecca who became monotheists before they were Muslims by adopting the faith of Abraham, the so-called *ḥanifiyya,* evidently a kind of pagan monotheism that is explicitly associated with Abraham in the third sura of the Qur'ān. Ubaydullāh reportedly emphasized to his former coreligionists that the transition from Islam to Christianity meant that

Muslims could see only half of what was before them, whereas Christians had a clear vision.[16]

Although Ubaydullāh divorced his wife after his conversion, and Muslim tradition, according to Ibn Iṣḥaq, claims that she then became a wife of the Prophet, Ubaydallāh himself, so far as can be told, suffered no penalty for apostasy at the hands of the Muslims. He sought no martyrdom, as some early Christians did after the advent of Islam. His integration into the Ethiopian polity and his acceptance by the Believers whom he left behind appear to anticipate Muslim tolerance of both Jews and Christians as "People of the Book" after the Islamic conquests. Although these non-Believers were subject to tax under Muslim authorities, as monotheists with their own sacred book they were neither persecuted nor executed for their beliefs. The consequences for conversion from Christianity to Islam would only be serious for anyone who chose subsequently to renounce Islam in order to return to the Christian fold. Such apostasy was viewed no less gravely than profaning the name and doctrines of Muḥammad, and it could unleash violent reprisals, including death.[17]

The impact of Christianity on the early Believers is mirrored in their regard for the *negus* in Ethiopia and their refuge in his kingdom. And this, in turn, had its roots in the long domination of the Ethiopians under Abraha in the Arabian peninsula. The Ethiopians had invaded the peninsula in 525 to bring an end to the abusive rule of Arab Jews, who had promoted their own monotheism by persecuting the Christians. When Abraha took over, the situation was inherently unstable, with the two monotheisms in opposition, and with a substantial core of pagans who had survived the incursions of monotheists of both kinds. When Abraha relinquished his kingdom to the Persians, Muḥammad inherited this religious volatility just as he started to proclaim Allāh as the one God. This was inevitably in opposition to the polytheists and yet, at the same time, in some kind of indeterminate relationship to the one God of the Christians and of the Jews. All of them had to acknowledge the piety of their common forefather, Abraham, a monotheist in a distant and irrecoverable time of universal paganism. Ethiopia was a significant link in this complex background of competing faiths.

Its recent experience in Arabia and with Arab refugees who had fled to Axum was part of a broader nexus that bound this Christian kingdom both to Byzantium and to the Jews. According to the legendary origins of the Ethiopians, the Ark of the

Covenant had miraculously arrived in Axum in the days of the Queen of Sheba.[18] This legend, which justified the belief, still current today, that the Ark is present in Ethiopia, had been duly enshrined in the holy book of Ethiopian Christianity, *The Glory of Kings (Kebra Nagast).* This work exists in a Ge'ez translation of an Arabic text that had itself been made from a Coptic version of a presumably Ge'ez original. The foundations of Ethiopic Christianity were laid down in the same Near Eastern milieu as the one that had allowed Muḥammad to launch his new monotheist religion.

5

THE PERSIANS IN JERUSALEM

In the fateful year 614 the armies of the Sassanian king Khosroes II set up siege-towers outside Jerusalem, breached its walls, and invaded the city. The invasion was the most devastating event to befall this ancient and holy city since the Roman forces had brought an end to the rebellion of Bar Kokhba in 135 and expelled the Jewish population. The Persians had made their way to Jerusalem after assaulting Syrian Antioch and moving southward by way of Caesarea-by-the-Sea. Apart from marauding monks, Samaritan uprisings, a minor disturbance under the Caesar Gallus, and the inconclusive mischief wrought by the apostate Julian, who wanted to rebuild the Temple, Palestine had not seen such violence or devastation for well over four centuries.

Although the Christian population grew in number over this period, the region had been generally hospitable to indigenous Jews, who flourished particularly in the Galilee and nourished an increasingly large cadre of rabbinical scholars. Traditional local pagan cults continued to flourish along with traditional Hellenism, which had led in late antiquity to the common use of the word "Hellene" simply to designate a pagan, although Greek language and culture maintained a distinct and prestigious existence alongside non-Greeks. The invasion of the Sassanian Persians delivered a shattering jolt to this relatively tranquil world after so many centuries and, in retrospect, it foreshadowed another great invasion just over two decades later. The parallel between the Persian capture of Jerusalem in 614 and the Muslim taking of the city in 638 naturally invites comparison and moralizing. But any connection between the two occupations would be tenuous at best and probably indefensible.

It will no longer do to claim that the Persian devastation left the region so physically, economically, and spiritually ruined that it was inevitably receptive to the armies of the Prophet, nor will it do to claim that the Muslims wiped out the vestiges of the old symbiosis of Jews, Christians, and pagans. What happened between 614 and 638 was undoubtedly disruptive and led, at the Battle of the Yarmuk in 636, to the end of Byzantine control of the region, but the wounds that Jerusalem and Palestine suffered were relatively slight and hardly altered the normal rhythms of daily life in both the countryside and the principal towns. It has gradually become apparent that the cultural, economic, and religious landscape did not look very much different after 638 from what it was before 614. The religious and ideological impulses behind the momentous upheavals of that period spawned, for centuries afterward, such varied and often contradictory narratives of what had just happened that only the most fastidious historical source criticism can make sense of it all.[1] Archaeology provides a much more reliable guide to what was going on, even if it appears to subvert the written historical record that was composed much later.[2]

The Persian arrival in Jerusalem had its ultimate origin in the murder of the Byzantine emperor Maurice in 602 through the intrigue of the usurper Phocas. The Shah of Persia, Khosroes II, had owed his throne to the favorable intercession of Maurice at a difficult time, and so, when Maurice was removed by a usurper, Khosroes rightly saw an opportunity to avenge his benefactor's death by taking advantage of the new weakness of the Byzantine Empire. He began a formidable campaign of aggression that constituted the greatest incursion of Persian forces into

Syria, Asia Minor, and Palestine since the conquests of Shapur I in the third century. The dormant hostility of the Sassanians, which Maurice had successfully used to his own advantage, now became terrifyingly active.

Khosroes's initiative not only opened the way for the removal of Phocas by the exceptionally astute Heraclius in 610, it brought the two empires into direct conflict under the personal leadership of their emperors. In 613 Khosroes inflicted a crushing defeat upon Heraclius in Asia Minor. He subsequently moved on into Syrian Antioch, which had barely recovered from the devastation of a Persian sack of the city in 540.[3] The taking of Antioch was an ominous prelude to the taking of Jerusalem in the following year.

Up to the moment of Maurice's death, the Sassanian Empire, which had long been Byzantium's rival in the Near and Middle East, had been quiescent during the overt expansionism of Justinian, and the two empires had pursued their interests obliquely by supporting client tribes such as the Jafnids (or Ghassānids) in Syria and the Naṣrids (or Lakhmids) in the South. In the Arabian peninsula the Persians had, as we have seen, brilliantly exploited the ambitions of the Arab converts to Judaism in Ḥimyar. With the rise of a strong king in Ethiopia who promoted an irredentist claim to recover former Ethiopian dominions in Arabia, the Christian *negus* in Axum had been able to further his ambitions by coming to the aid of Christians across the Red Sea during a cruel persecution at the hands of the Jewish Ḥimyarites. This gave the Persians an opportunity to reassert their support of the Jews in opposition to the Christians, whose final operations in the Arabian peninsula had received explicit encouragement from the Byzantine emperor.[4]

By the time that the army of Khosroes stood outside the walls of Jerusalem it could hardly have been a secret that Jews had every reason to expect the support of the invaders. The record of Persian sympathy for Jews in the Arabian peninsula was firmly on record, and it is likely that Jewish Ḥimyarites in Palestine, such as those whose tombs have been found at Bet She'arim, would have been well aware of what their co-religionists owed to the Persians.[5] Not far from Jerusalem itself the recently discovered epitaph for a certain Leah points to an even closer link to the Holy City. It has a bilingual text, starting with a quotation from *Daniel,* in mixed Aramaic and Hebrew, and, below it, a text in South Arabian Sabaic.[6]

It is clear from two surviving texts that were composed within a few decades of 614 that the Jews were not disappointed in any hopes they may have placed in the Persian invaders, and that the Jews in Jerusalem, for their part, did what they could to support the Persian presence. Despite the Babylonian Captivity, and long after it, the Jews had been a major presence in Mesopotamia, and it is not altogether surprising that the Jews in Jerusalem in 614 cooperated willingly with the Persian invaders. Two eyewitness sources fill out the picture of what happened.

The first of these was written by a monk of Mar Saba after the recovery of the True Cross by Heraclius in 630. He bore the name of Strategios, although this name has, in recent scholarship, sometimes been illicitly annexed to that of a ghostly author called Antiochus or Antiochius, whom Migne's *Patrologia Graeca* patched together long ago from various texts. There is no doubt that Strategios was not Antiochus or Antiochius and that he wrote his narrative originally in Greek. But, unfortunately for us, we know it only from Georgian and Arabic translations. The Georgian tradition is more reliable and certainly better edited.[7] Strategios's narrative is undoubtedly hyperbolic in places, but it is marvelously circumstantial, with many topographical details concerning recognizable places in Jerusalem as well as an explicit reference to the monk Modestus, whose correspondence with the Armenian Katholikos Komitas guarantees his historicity. Strategios strangely blamed the fate of the Christians in Jerusalem on the city's circus factions, the Blues and the Greens, because he saw the Persian invasion as a divine penalty for sin and blamed the factions for leading the Christian population astray. Strategios's reports of massacres and communal burials, as well as his claims of Persian destruction of churches and shrines, necessarily require the sober control of archaeology, and this has only recently become possible.

But, before turning to that as well as to the second eyewitness source, we need to take a closer look at Strategios's account. Here is what he reports:

> The vicious Jews, both enemies of truth and haters of Christ, greatly rejoiced as they saw the Christians handed over into the hands of the enemy. They conceived an evil plan in accordance with their ill will towards the people, for they had acquired a great reputation with the Persians as the betrayers of Christians. At that time they were standing by the edge of a reservoir and shouting to the sons of God, who were detained there, and they said to them, "If you want to avoid death, become Jews and deny

> Christ. Come up from there and come to us. We will buy you back from the Persians with our money, and you will thereby benefit through us." The wicked intent of their plan was not carried out, and their effort turned out to be in vain. For the sons of the holy Church chose to die for Christ rather than to live impiously.[8]

This narrative is plainly anti-Jewish. Although there is no explicit assertion that the Persians had been predisposed to favor the Jews, that is the unmistakable implication. Strategios also mentions another religious constituency in the city, namely the pagans, whom he calls, in conformity with current usage of the time, Greeks (Hellenes). These people he accuses of cowardice. The monk Modestus had tried to mobilize an army of so-called Greeks to help, but as soon as those poor souls had taken a look at the size of the Persian force, they fled.[9] Hence the Greeks who bolted must have been local pagans. Strategios also refers to "inhabitants of the city" who were distressed by the flight of the Greeks before the Persians, and these might well have been pagans whom Modestus had not recruited. Neither the Jews nor the pagans appear to receive the slightest sympathy from the

Christians, even though Strategios believed that it was the Christians who had brought the whole catastrophe upon themselves through their wanton behavior as fans of the circus factions. His entire interpretation, to say nothing of his language for the various communities in the city, is open to debate, but it would be reasonable to infer that the Persians had demonstrated both support of the Jews and indifference toward the pagans. The Byzantine Christians were their target.

At more or less the same time as Strategios was writing, a second eyewitness report came from the monk and future patriarch Sophronius, who was engaged in the composition of a series of twenty-two bravura poems in Greek and in the classical Anacreontic meter to celebrate liturgical feasts. Sophronius, who was also known as a sophist, was steeped in the Greek poetic tradition, and his twenty-two Anacreontic poems (no. 23 is rightly considered spurious) include a piece on the Persian capture of Jerusalem as well as two others on the city's holy places.[10] It is unknown whether Sophronius was actually in the city in 614, although he certainly had been there and was briefly in Alexandria later with his friend John Moschus. He left Alexandria for Rome with Moschus, who died there.

The fourteenth of Sophronius's Anacreontic poems is entirely devoted to the capture of the Holy City, and, like Strategios's account, it appears to be based on personal experience, or at least on direct testimony from an eyewitness. It inveighs mercilessly against the Sassanian invaders, who are called not only Persians, but also, derogatively, Medes and Parthians. Sophronius's language is dramatic: "The treacherous Mede arrived from wicked Persia, fighting cities and citizens, fighting the lord of Rome [this means Byzantium]. . . . A daemon has arisen with angry fury and murderous intent, destroying many holy cities with bloody swords." The poem moves on to the Jews: "When they [the Christians] saw the Parthians [*sic*] at hand together with their Jewish friends, they ran off at once and fastened the gates of the city"—to pray for Christ's help. Sophronius died in 638 after serving as the patriarch of Jerusalem for the previous four years. This was the year in which the Muslims arrived. It was his last year as patriarch, and it was he who made the pact with the Muslim Caliph 'Umar al Khaṭṭāb to turn over Jerusalem to the Arabs.[11]

If we can find some kind of historical explanation for the role of Jews during the capture of Jerusalem in 614, even after discounting the tendentiousness of Strategios's account, we are still left with a wealth of topographical details about mass burials and devastated churches. These details have long dominated modern accounts of the capture of the city. Yet the numbers of the Christian dead are given in the tens of thousands, a figure that is intrinsically improbable. The Nea Church of the Theotokos, the Church of Holy Zion, the Church of the Probatica, the Church of the Holy Sepulchre, as well as churches on the Mount of Olives figure prominently. Many of these sites appear, with an appeal to archaeological remains, in the comprehensive introduction to Jerusalem's history at the beginning of the first volume of the new *Corpus* of inscriptions of Judaea and Palestine.[12] But it is to Gideon Avni that we now owe a definitive report on such archaeological evidence as there is for both mass burials and the destruction of churches. With data and support supplied by many of his colleagues, he has constructed a powerful case against the historical value of much of Strategios's testimony, without, as in Strategios's comments on the Jews, rejecting it altogether.[13]

Avni observes that a certain Thomas, according to Strategios, organized the burial of the Christian dead in Jerusalem in thirty-five different locations. Although some of these locations can be correlated with known sites, careful archaeological examination of the stratigraphy either shows no evidence for destruction layers at the time of the Persian invasion or the lack of ceramic materials that might be used to date any burnt layers. As for actual burials, only seven sites of Byzantine date have been discovered, and these are all outside the Old City. The one secure correlation with information in Strategios occurs in the case of a rock-cut cave in Mamilla, some 120 meters west of the Jaffa Gate. Strategios states that masses of Christians who assembled at Mamilla were massacred and that the pious Thomas removed their corpses to a nearby cave. The cave that has been excavated at Mamilla did indeed prove to contain human bones, and a small chapel in front of it was decorated with Christian symbols, including three crosses. Anthropological analysis of the bones has suggested that most of the hundreds of skeletons in the cave were the remains of young persons, with women outnumbering men. Avni writes, "All this suggests that the deceased met a sudden death."[14]

In the Mamilla cave as well as in the six other mass burials of the same period, the method of burial, as Avni has stressed, is very different from other Byzantine burials in Jerusalem. These were normally in spaces devoted to a family or in crypts within the grounds of a monastery. So the seven mass burials are undoubtedly exceptional, indicating a hasty removal of corpses and reasonably pointing to the time of the Persian invasion. With that said, it is nevertheless clear that the deaths and sepulchres are far fewer than Strategios has described, and this encourages skepticism about his reports of the devastation of buildings, especially churches. Despite previous claims of archaeological evidence for this devastation, Avni stresses that the interpretations were inaccurate because there was no reasonable ceramic classification to provide a credible chronology. The recent and extensive analysis carried out by Jodi Magness now reveals a remarkable continuity of pottery types as well as coins, and this has suggested to many historians in recent years an uninterrupted occupation across and beyond the Persian conquest, as well as the Islamic.[15]

Robert Schick has emphasized, in his invaluable work on the Christian communities of Palestine, that the Church of the Holy Sepulchre is often said to have been set on fire and seriously damaged, providing an opportunity for the holy Modestus to make major repairs with the help of donations from the pious. But we now know that there was no significant damage to the church in the early seventh century, nor were there any substantial repairs or renovations.[16] Thanks to Leah Di Segni's analysis of monograms inscribed on the Byzantine capitals of the church, we learn that the emperor Maurice installed the capitals during repairs at the end of the sixth century.[17] They were left untouched by the Persian invaders. Similarly, Avni has demolished the archaeological conclusions for destruction at the Church of Holy Zion as well as the Eleona and Gethsemane on the Mount of Olives.

It will always be conceivable that whatever damage the Persians did in Jerusalem was so rapidly repaired that no traces remained, but the odds are against this. Strategios clearly exaggerated both the numbers of the dead and the location of mass burials. Recent excavations on the northwest side of the City of David hill provide an instructive modification of this less sensational interpretation. A hoard of 264 mint-condition gold coins has been discovered in what seems to have been an administrative building. These coins are unique, representing a hitherto unknown variant of Heraclius's coinage as it is known between 610 and 613. The 264 unexampled coins, all including a particularly egregious error in which the first letter of Heraclius's Latin name appears as an A rather than an H, look to excavators, with good reason, as if they were struck locally in a temporary mint in Jerusalem that was set up to provide cash for the Byzantine occupation force. If so, the hoard represents a desperate effort to salvage the money when the building itself was destroyed, as it seems to have been. Because the date would evidently be soon after 613, we may well have in this new discovery a trace of the Persian invasion in 614, but if so, this was clearly not a violation of a sacred building. The scholars who have published their findings on the new hoard reasonably ask whether the coins might have come from a Byzantine treasury used for paying troops, and that might be precisely why the Persians wanted to break up the building.[18] Holy places and sectarian struggles do not seem to have had the slightest part in Persian action at the site, and to that extent the new excavations, while documenting destruction in 614, in no way alter the picture that archaeologists have constructed in the last few years of Jerusalem's tombs and churches.

In fact, the picture that has now emerged of the Holy City after the Persians moved on into Egypt bears a startling resemblance to one that Clive Foss sketched more than a decade ago for all the places through which the armies of Khosroes II marched after the usurpation of Phocas. It had been customary to assume that the Persian invasion wiped out the civilization of the region, as well as its agriculture, its cities, and its trade, and this apocalyptic vision not only informed subsequent scholarship but led archaeologists to interpret their data in accordance with it. The devastation of the Persian invasion seemed to many to have facilitated the early Islamic conquests. But this interpretation can now be seen to have been simply wrong.[19]

While acknowledging that the various fragmentary chronicles upon which historians rely often suggest that Persian rule "was a disaster for the local populations, featuring bloodshed and extraordinary exactions," Foss meticulously documented the systematic retention of local administrative structures by the Persians and the modest scope of their more violent acts, usually in response to resistance. His work has now been superseded and fully confirmed by the magisterial book that Gideon Avni has published on the "Byzantine-Islamic transition" in Palestine.[20]

To judge from southern Syria, the outlying regions of Palestine reveal normal activity continuing through the Persian occupation, with numerous inscriptions dated to the period 614–630. This drastically revised account of the Persian invasion in the seventh century has engendered a new consensus about the Near East on the eve of the Islamic conquests. Instead of lying desolate and ready for new rulers, it was already experienced in survival under a foreign power and therefore all the more likely to be accommodating when a new one arrived. Since the Persians generally supported the Monophysites, they were able to maintain their struggle against Byzantium in a doctrinal way that was not unlike their support of the Jews in Jerusalem in their opposition to the Chalcedonian Christians they found in the city. Certainly the Christians suffered grievously, but there is little indication that either the Jews or the pagans did.

The most significant aftermath of the Persian capture of Jerusalem was the occupation of Egypt. Alexandria had already received many Chalcedonian refugees, who had been unhappy in Palestine with an alien administration that supported Monophysites, but the arrival of the Persians in Egypt exiled these Chalcedonians yet again. Such a dedicated Christian as John the Almsgiver, Orthodox patriarch of Alexandria from 610 to 617, chose to leave his flock and flee to Cyprus, where he died in 619. Even the future patriarch of Jerusalem, Sophronius, who had recently come to Alexandria and had written—or would soon write—such eloquent verses about the capture of the city, decamped as well for Rome. The Persians cleverly exploited the confessional confusion of Near

Eastern Christendom in their war against Byzantium. This meant that the brunt of the invasion fell upon the Chalcedonians and the emperor Heraclius, against whom the Sassanians were waging their war. But in pacifying and administering the regions they had conquered, they created a world that was not much different from what it had been before, with its rich traditions of Judaism, Christianity, and Hellenism (understood as both religion and culture).

Accordingly when the armies of Muḥammad eventually arrived, they did not find a shattered civilization and a ruined economy. They found Christian communities that the previous invaders had supported, as well as Chalcedonians like Sophronius, who had returned peacefully to Jerusalem in 619 after the death of his friend John Moschus. At some point, once he had returned from his exile in Alexandria, Sophronius included among his Anacreontic poems on church feasts not only his bitter lamentation over the Persian invasion of 614, but two other poems, which were a detailed and nostalgic celebration of the city's principal monuments and holy places. Exactly when he wrote these poems is unclear, but we can be sure that he was back in Jerusalem by 619. He had either experienced the events of 614 in person or was well informed about them, but five years later he must have observed with his own eyes the state of the city at that time. Since he is unlikely to have been composing elaborate Greek verses when Moschus was dying in Rome, the odds are that the Anacreontics about the glories of Jerusalem were written after he had actually returned to the city. The poems themselves imply, by their impassioned longing to see the various monuments, that he was away when he was writing them, but perhaps, by a familiar literary artifice, he imagined his nostalgia after he was back in the city. In any case, absolutely nothing in the two poems about the holy places of Jerusalem suggests that Sophronius was aware, either from autopsy or report, of the slightest damage or destruction to any of them.

Meanwhile, the Arabs in Arabia showed little interest in the quarrels of Monophysites and Chalcedonians, and there was no reason why they should have. They could remember that the Monophysite *negus* of Ethiopia had gladly made common cause with the Chalcedonian emperor in Constantinople, and, more importantly, that refugees from the civil strife in the Prophet's city of Mecca had fled for safety to Axum. At the moment of Mohammed's own emigration *(hijra)* from Mecca to Medina in 622, the superpowers of the Near East were still Sassanian Persia and the Byzantine Empire—which was known everywhere in the region as Rome. One of these two was soon to be annihilated. Neither of them could possibly have expected this to happen. Neither did Muḥammad and his successors.

6

MUḤAMMAD AND MEDINA

DURING THE TIME of the revelations to Muḥammad at Mecca, the opposition he provoked within his own tribe of the Quraysh inevitably clouded his mission and influence. The exodus of his supporters to the Christian kingdom in Axum not only reflected the trouble at home but the common bond that monotheism had forged between a new prophet, who proclaimed himself the Messenger of the one God, and the much older and deeply rooted monotheist faiths. A circumambient cloud of other monotheist prophets that emerged in Arabia at the same time as Muḥammad provided competitors for him, but these movements utterly lacked the deep roots of the older monotheist religions. These were precisely two in the ancient Mediterranean world: one was Christianity, which was the religion of Byzantium and Ethiopia, in its Chalcedonian and non-Chalcedonian (Monophysite or, or in more current terminology, Miaphysite) forms, and the other was Judaism, in both Judaea itself and the Jewish diaspora from North Africa to Iraq.

The Jews were no strangers to the Arabs of the peninsula. After the destruction of the Temple in Jerusalem at the hands of Vespasian and Titus in 70, the exodus from the city vastly enlarged the Jewish diaspora and brought the faith of Israel to the notice of Arabs well before the spread of Christian monotheism in the centuries that followed. Some Jewish communities appear to have settled in southern Yemen and along the coast of the Ḥaḍramawt, where one or two early synagogues can be recognized. An undated and undatable inscription in Hebrew script from Bait al-Ḥāḍir near Tanʿim east of Ṣanʿāʾ lists the twenty-four names of traditional *mishmarōt* (priestly divisions or wards) for service in the Temple, and, despite its many problems, it bears witness to a deep attachment to the Land of Israel. A graffito from Qāniʾ suggests a relatively early Jewish community and possibly a synagogue on the southern coast of the peninsula.[1] But possibly the most substantial emigration to Arabia after 70 was the core of the Jewish community for which evidence can be found in the northwestern Ḥijāz, at Yathrib, principally in the upper and more attractive part of that oasis. In territory that was well watered and good for agriculture, the Jews of Yathrib became arguably the most entrenched representatives of monotheism in pre-Islamic Arabia.[2] Their message and ritual observances attracted both attention and imitation.

Jewish monotheism acquired a militant character when, surprisingly and for reasons that are still unclear, the Arab kings of Ḥimyar espoused it in the later fourth century, precisely when Christianity reached both Arabia and Ethiopia. The struggle between these two monotheisms, one of which had been born from the womb of the other, gave an almost fratricidal aspect to their struggles in the fifth and sixth centuries. The Jewish Arabs of Ḥimyar embarked upon a merciless campaign of persecution wherever Christians had settled. The bloody massacre of Christians that the Ḥimyarites carried out at Najrān in 523 was known to both the Persians and the Christians outside Arabia through the boasting of Yūsuf, the king who carried it out. His vicious assault on the Christians of Najrān created an ominous precedent for the future.[3]

The long-standing conflict between the Christian Byzantines and the Zoroastrian Sassanians in Persia would now be played out in Arabia by proxy—first through Ethiopian intervention, with the assistance of the Byzantines in support of their Christian brethren in Arabia, and second through Persian support of the Jews, particularly by way of their Naṣrid clients at al-Ḥīra, where a Jewish community seems to have preceded the Christian one.[4] The two great monotheisms of pre-Islamic late antiquity, which had been rooted in Arabia for at least three centuries, continued to flourish after the defeat of the Ḥimyarite Jews. Although both religions proved to be ineradicable, they were unstable components of Arabian society before Muḥammad. The emigration of the Prophet's followers to Axum belongs in this context.

Meanwhile, by the time Muḥammad was born in about 570, which was well after the suppression of the Jewish monarchy in Ḥimyar and the subsequent collapse of the Ethiopian Christian monarchy of Abraha that succeeded it, the peninsula lay open for the Sassanian Persians to assume remote control of Arabian affairs with the help of their Naṣrid clients. When the Messenger of God at Mecca found himself increasingly troubled by domestic opposition, as well as isolated through the emigration of some of his Believers to Axum, an exceptional opportunity arose for various interested parties in the oasis of Yathrib, some 200 miles to the north, to secure and to improve their diplomatic and economic positions. They seized upon the instability that had broken out in the region as the mission of Muḥammad was gathering strength.

A reconfiguration of the political and religious kaleidoscope suddenly became possible, and neither Byzantium nor Baghdad could ignore this possibility. It is clear that neither did. The Jews of Yathrib were, as they had long been, an influential and relatively affluent part of the city, but in recent decades they had come into conflict with two pagan tribes that had moved into the city within the preceding century. These were the powerful Khazraj and Aws. Their interaction with the Jews at this time had momentous implications for the location and nature of the mission of Muḥammad.

The tribes of the Khazraj and the rival but much less populous Aws were still predominantly pagan, although the faith of the Believers in Mecca had begun to win converts. These two tribes occupied the lower part of Yathrib by virtue of their arrival long after the Jews, who had taken over the more desirable upper city. But the covetous interest of the Khazraj in the sweet water and arable land that belonged to the Jews inevitably led to hostility and conflict that culminated in a battle at Buʿāth in about 617.[5] In this encounter the Aws fought alongside the Jews because of their animosity toward the much larger pagan tribe of the Khazraj. In the following years the message that Muḥammad's Believers were making known won more converts among the pagans, and nowhere more than among the restless and dissatisfied people of the Khazraj. These new Believers at Yathrib are named in later Muslim sources as "helpers" to the cause, *anṣār*, and in June of 622 a good seventy of them went to ʿAqaba, during the pilgrimage season, to propose to Muḥammad that he escape from his difficulties in Mecca by emigrating, together with his Believers, to join the *anṣār* in Yathrib.

Before the year was over, this was exactly what Muḥammad did. His momentous *hijra* in 622 provided the starting point for Muslim chronology forever afterward, and it inaugurated a new phase in the Prophet's revelations, during which the Quranic texts become ever more verbose. Yathrib henceforth changed its name to the simple word for a city, Medina, and those parts of the Qur'ān that were revealed there became known as the Medinan suras. How it happened that the Khazraj were able to organize the invitation to Muḥammad, and to facilitate the reception of his followers in a city with a substantial Jewish population that had recently been allied with the Aws, remains today an event that is as mysterious as it is almost certainly historical. How Medina managed to adapt to its new immigrant population of Believers is equally obscure, but it manifestly did.

There can be no doubt that a fusion of Jews, pagan Khazraj, pagan Aws, and Meccan Believers within Medina soon took place without any evident resistance. The proof of this fusion lies unmistakably in the famous document that was drawn up to establish the rights and privileges of the newly combined community *(ʿumma),* a document that is often called the Constitution of Medina. If there is one documentary text from the lifetime of the Prophet that nearly all scholars acknowledge to be authentic, it is this one.[6] Its language is so different from that of the later traditions in which it is embedded that its authenticity gleams brilliantly amid the voluminous accretions in which it survives. It lays out parallel rights and privileges for the Jews of the city, for the Khazraj, the Aws, and a few other groups that lived in Medina. The resolution, by constitutional settlement, of the reorganization caused by the *hijra* cannot conceivably have occurred without the consent of the Khazraj in concerted action with the Jews, and above all with those very Jewish tribes (Naḍīr and Qurayẓa) that the Aws had joined at the Battle of Buʿāth some five years earlier.

The astonishing agreement that is represented in the *ʿumma* document points to a comparable agreement that initiated the whole process of bringing the

Believers into the city in the first place. It must have been obvious to the Khazraj, Aws, and Jews in 622 that Muḥammad was in trouble at Mecca, but it is less obvious why the Jews as well as the pagan Khazraj and Aws would have joined forces with the believing *anṣār* to invite him into their city.

Michael Lecker has recently suggested a solution to this problem that is as bold as it is attractive.[7] It is very likely to be correct because it addresses both the self-interest and political diplomacy of the several parties to the agreement at the same time as invoking their religious and tribal allegiances from an international perspective that encompasses both Byzantium and Persia. The link that Lecker proposes in order to bring all this together into a coherent explanation of the *hijra* is a supervenient role for Byzantium's Arab clients, the Jafnid dynasty of the tribal alliance of Ghassānids. These Arabs served the emperor in Constantinople in exactly the same way as the Naṣrid dynasty of the Lakhmids at al-Hīra served the shah in Baghdad. Since both Byzantium and Persia had a history of exercising their influence in Arabia through clients in the region, it is not unreasonable to look for intervention from outside Arabia in the momentous events of 622.

Lecker begins with a straightforward observation of a remarkable coincidence—a coincidence so obvious that it is astonishing to find that it has failed to engage the attention of most historians of the *hijra.* The year of the *hijra,* 622, was precisely the year in which the Byzantine emperor Heraclius began his military onslaught on the Persian Empire. This was an operation that terminated, after various supplementary campaigns (including one against the Avars), with his audacious invasion of 628 deep into the Mesopotamian heartland of the Persian Empire. Heraclius's bold and brilliant move was the beginning of the end of the Shah Khosroes and of the Sassanian Empire that had taken shape four centuries earlier. A connection between the *hijra* of Muḥammad and Heraclius's launch of his great offensive might well be indicated by the occurrence of both in the same year. With the Ghassānids at his disposal, Heraclius, who was an exceptionally astute strategist, could have discerned an opportunity for weakening the Persian enemy on his Arabian flank.

Heraclius must have known from Arabian history of the sixth century that his Persian antagonists supported the Jews, much as the Byzantines supported the Christians, and it was no secret that the Jewish population of Medina was among the most significant community of Jews in northwestern Arabia. The city was not far removed from the famous palm groves that Justinian's Palestinian phylarch Abū Karib had grandly turned over to the emperor. Although these palm groves were not of great value, they constituted a territory that lay between Palestine and the Ḥijāz.[8] They were therefore important for Byzantine influence in the area. In the early seventh century Heraclius cannot have been ignorant of what had been going on in Mecca and Axum with the revelations of Muḥammad and the emergence of the *anṣār* at Medina. He would certainly have seen in the city's Jewish population a political resource that the Persians might exploit against the Byzantine Christians. This was, after all, exactly what they had done when they captured Jerusalem in 614 by offering support to the Jews in the process of dislodging the Christians and their sacred relics.

In planning his Persian offensive in 622 Heraclius would have had every reason to ensure that the Persians would not stir up trouble in the Ḥijāz of the kind that they had already provoked in Palestine. It made perfect sense for him to turn to his Ghassānid clients to address this contingency, and what Lecker has now demonstrated is that those clients were in a position to influence the Khazraj and the Jews. He has meticulously noted the Ghassānid presence in groups that are listed in the Constitution of Medina, notably among both Khazraj and Jews. This link across the various tribes and religions would explain the otherwise puzzling cooperation of the pagans, *anṣār,* and Jews, after a recent history of hostility, in both the invitation to Muḥammad and the subsequent incorporation of the Believers into the community of Medina.

Neither Lecker nor anyone else will be able to describe, without fanciful embellishment, what arguments figured in the negotiations that brought these diverse groups together, first in welcoming the Believers and then in forging the Constitution document. But the presence of Ghassānids in very different ethnic and religious parts of the city would have encouraged the diffusion of a new polity across a wide spectrum within the frame of the Byzantine-Persian struggle. If Heraclius had indeed persuaded his Ghassānid clients to intercede with well-placed persons in Medina, this could have served to bring some measure of unity to what had long been a divided city, and it would have muted the enmities that were embroiling Mecca at the time. From Heraclius's perspective it would have served the valuable purpose of neutralizing the Jews in the event of any Persian effort to co-opt them. Above all it would have made it possible for Heraclius to launch his campaign against Khosroes at the very moment when Muḥammad and his Believers were decamping for a new homeland.

Meanwhile, in the years before Heraclius finally made his decisive invasion of Mesopotamia in 628, Muḥammad, from the relative security of his new base in Medina, undertook to deal with the enemies he had left behind in Mecca. Trouble had arisen soon after his move to the great oasis to the north of his own city, and some of his emigrant Believers raided a caravan on its way to Mecca at Nakhla during a sacred month when violence should have been forbidden. This aggression was soon followed, in 624, by a successful assault on Meccan protectors of a caravan at Badr. In the next year the Meccans retaliated with an attack on Medina itself, just as Muḥammad's relations with the Jews of the city had turned sour on suspicion that the Naḍīr clan, in collusion with hostile Meccans, was conspiring to kill him. Consequently many of those Jews decamped from Medina to the oasis of Khaybar farther north.

The spiraling deterioration of the position of the Believers in Medina led the Meccan opposition to lay siege to Medina. To safeguard themselves, the Believers surrounded themselves with a trench *(ukhdūd)* that became legendary in Muslim tradition as the scene of a Meccan retreat, which was commemorated in Sura 85 of the Qur'ān. Taking advantage of this success, Muḥammad directed his ire and followers against another Jewish tribe, the Qurayẓa, which he believed to have been in contact with the Meccans. After an aborted attempt to enter Mecca in 628 to perform the lesser pilgrimage known as the *'umra,* Muḥammad and his Believers reached an agreement at Ḥudaybiya, on the outskirts of Mecca.[9] This was to authorize the *'umra* in the next year and to assure a ten-year truce between both sides.

There is general agreement among historians that the Ḥudaybiya settlement gave Muḥammad the crucial advantage he needed, not only to root out the Jews who had retreated to Khaybar but, more significantly, to move against the Quraysh at Mecca with an army in 630. This marked the end of the resistance of the Quraysh through their espousal of the new faith. More dramatically, it allowed Muḥammad to cleanse his own city of its surviving pagan vestiges. He did this by conspicuously removing the pagan images from the Ka'ba and laying claim to the monotheist origins of the shrine as preserved in the story that Abraham had built it. The year 630 was a critical moment in the career of the Prophet and the ascendancy of Islam. He was now strong enough to counter the tribal opposition that continued outside Mecca, notably at Ṭā'if to the south. That city surrendered to him after a siege. But only two years later the Prophet was dead.

Like many great leaders and visionaries, Muḥammad had done little to prepare for the moment when he would no longer be there to guide and inspire his Believers. The movement he started had reached a dangerous moment, when many of those who had supported him might now aspire to succeed him. It would require nearly three decades before the Umayyad dynasty would take firm control of the Islamic empire at Damascus in 661. Those three decades constituted the final stage in the forging of Islam as we know it. They were also the time of the greatest uncertainty about the future of the Prophet's mission.

7

INTERREGNUM OF THE FOUR CALIPHS

THE DEATH OF Muḥammad in 632 brought a sudden and perilous instability to the structure of Islamic government that had taken shape after the conquests that occupied the last years of the Prophet's life. Muslim tradition includes reports that suggest he may actually have led his armies into battle for a year or two after the canonical date of his death, but assiduous probing of the possibility that he lived beyond 632 has failed to convince most historians.[1] Muḥammad had designated no successor, but his followers managed to agree in appointing his chief assistant Abū Bakr to take over as the leader of the Believers *(amīr al-mu'minim)*. He survived a mere two years, but these were the years of the so-called Apostasy Wars *(ridda)*, which attempted to exploit the insecurity that followed Muḥammad's death. It is important to remember that rival monotheist prophets, who had already challenged him in his lifetime, Musaylima above all, became increasingly active in this uncertain time, and both in Yamāma in central Arabia and in Yemen they posed a threat of rear-guard action that Abū Bakr was obliged to address. At that moment the supremacy of the Believers as the sole custodians of Arab monotheism was by no means assured.

But the end of the *ridda* in 633 allowed Abū Bakr to open fronts on either side of the Jordan Valley, one in Palestine through the Negev in the direction of Gaza under the leadership of ʿAmr ibn al-Āṣ, and a correlative campaign in central and northern Transjordan. At the same time Abū Bakr sent his general Khālid ibn al Walīd into southern Iraq to confront the Sassanians. These three operations, soon after Muḥammad's death, reflected the necessity to secure for his followers those territories that were subject to Byzantium to their west and to Persia to their east. Abū Bakr died in 634 after a mere two years as the first of four Medinan leaders, each of whom the tradition reasonably identifies henceforth as a caliph or successor *(khalīfa)*. It fell to Abū Bakr and the next three caliphs after the Prophet's death to lay claim to Syria, Palestine, and Iraq, as well as Egypt and Libya, well before the establishment of the Umayyad dynasty at Damascus in 661.

Despite the extreme paucity of contemporary sources, two texts from the years immediately after Muḥammad's death provide confirmation of the invasions carried out by his followers. They both refer to events of 634 and cannot have been written much later. One is in Syriac, with reference to "the Arabs of Muḥammad," and the other is in Greek, with reference to "the prophet coming with the Saracens."[2] Although these brief allusions might be taken as indicating that Muḥammad was still alive in 634 and leading his forces, the obvious and most widely accepted interpretation is simply that his inspiration for the invasions led the Syriac and Greek authors to refer to him as a living presence. At the least they offer testimony that is closer than anything else to contemporary documentation for Muḥammad's historical existence, which, like so much in the history of this time, has been questioned.

Abū Bakr and his successors were responsible for launching and carrying through these conquests not only in a relatively brief time but with almost no disruption in the daily life of the region. It has become apparent from archaeological study in recent years that what was always recognized to have been an exceptionally swift, and sometimes invisible, conquest, was above all a nonviolent one. As Gideon Avni has written, "the gap between the historical narratives and the archaeological evidence is striking." In addition to taking over extensive land, together with cities, churches, synagogues, and pagan shrines, Abū Bakr in two years set a model for the caliphs that were to succeed him through his three major achievements: he eliminated the cloud of other prophets that had contested Muḥammad during his lifetime, he challenged Byzantium in its control of Palestine and Syria, and he challenged Persia in its control of Iraq. All these military successes were combined with invasions that, at least for the local people, involved very little change in the conduct of daily affairs from what they had known before. The principal innovation was the imposition on residents of the occupied territory of the *jizya,* or "head tax," which largely served to compensate the soldiers, and a tax on land *(kharāj).*[3]

Otherwise the landscape, both economic and physical, was barely altered in these early years of conquest. No new coinage was introduced. Churches, synagogues, and pagan shrines were left exactly as they were, together with the visible relics of their cults—mosaics, paintings, sculpture, and architecture. Some churches, as, for example, two at Rihab in Jordan about 635, were being built or renovated even as the conquests were taking place.[4] At Khirbet al-Samrā new mosaic floors were being laid in its churches in 635 and 640. The Islamic conquests were by no means devastating and accommodated the culture and the faiths of much of the region over which the Muslims took control.

Yet under the leadership of the second caliph, ʿUmar ibn al-Khaṭṭāb, the Muslim army in southern Syria was able to win a decisive battle against the forces of Heraclius in 636 at the river Yarmuk, and this allowed the nascent administration of those who may now be properly called Muslims to turn back to southern Palestine and Egypt, on their western flank, and to Sassanian Iraq on their eastern. Sophronius, the patriarch of Jerusalem, watched with concern but not with alarm the advance of ʿUmar's army into Bethlehem, and, in one of the most remarkable and indicative episodes in early Islamic history, he personally welcomed ʿUmar when he arrived in Jerusalem in 638. Active resistance to the invaders was relatively rare, except at Caesarea-by-the-Sea, which held out during an off-and-on siege over seven years. Those years finally ended in reported casualties. But it is more than likely that the Christian historian Theophanes, writing in the ninth century, exaggerated them.[5]

By comparison with the great battle at the Yarmuk two years before, the success of the Muslims in taking Jerusalem by a diplomatic agreement without any bloodshed was the achievement of two men, Sophronius and ʿUmar. The surrender of the city in 638 could not have been more different from its capitulation to the Persians twenty-four years before, when the city was taken by armed assault with the collaboration of the Jewish residents. The patriarch and the caliph must have carefully calculated the impact on their respective constituencies, namely the Byzantine Christians and the invading Muslims. After the Persian capture of the city in 614 the Christians had been dispossessed, and the relics of the True Cross removed to Baghdad. But by 638 the Christians were back, thanks to Heraclius, and it seems clear that ʿUmar had no interest in expelling them a second time. Nor did Sophronius show the slightest interest in excluding the Muslims. He agreed to provide immunity for Arabs in the territory but ensured that the Jews, whose former collaboration with the Persians was only too well known, would be kept out. Both Christians and Muslims seemed more concerned to negotiate a peaceful transfer of power than to precipitate a confrontation.

The reason why this should have been so, not long after the catastrophe at the Yarmuk, should be sought in the desire of both Palestinian Christians and incoming Muslims to take over, with minimal alteration, the pre-existing organization of the region, and to allow daily life to continue as before. That desire was most probably rooted in the recognition that both sides were strongly monotheist, and that both clearly acknowledged Jerusalem as the Holy City, al-Quds. The exclusion of Jews, the other monotheist "People of the Book," as the Qur'ān called them, though undoubtedly due to their long-standing alliance with the Persians, did not in any way diminish the holiness of Jerusalem in Muslim eyes. Initially prayers were directed to Jerusalem. Only later did Mecca become the orientation for prayer, but this came after a transitional period in which two prayer niches *(qiblatain)* appeared in some mosques, one facing Jerusalem and one facing Mecca. On occasion even churches were called into service for Muslim observances.[6] The lack of alarm in Sophronius's acceptance of the Arabs in Bethlehem foreshadowed the diplomatic agreement that he reached when 'Umar actually entered Jerusalem.

The earliest surviving account of 'Umar's arrival in the city is demonstrably the most prejudicial and the least reliable. It appears in the *Chronographia* of the ninth-century Christian Greek historian Theophanes

Confessor, who reflects a later and strongly Christian condemnation of the Muslim presence.[7] The caliph is depicted as a barbarian wearing filthy garments that he is unwilling to exchange for clean ones until he is assured that he can recover his own just as soon as they are washed. Theophanes highlights his interest in praying on the site of the Jewish Temple, in order to provide yet another example of his barbarism. According to Theophanes, Sophronius is even said to have exclaimed, upon hearing of ʿUmar's interest in building a mosque where the Temple had been, that this was truly "the abomination of desolation." These were the apocalyptic words of the prophet Daniel that Jesus is reported to have invoked, according to the Gospels of Matthew and Mark, in allusion to the forthcoming destruction of the Temple.[8]

But sources in both Arabic and Syriac, despite being later in date than Theophanes, have now been proven conclusively to contain very different accounts that conspicuously antedate what Theophanes reports in his Greek history.[9] These accounts agree in depicting ʿUmar as a humble and simple man, whose modest attire reflected his modest character. Maria Conterno has shown, through meticulous comparison of the sources, that this unprejudiced account of ʿUmar's arrival in Jerusalem reflects, in all probability, reports that were either contemporary with the events or were circulated soon afterward and subsequently written down in Greek before being incorporated into the Syriac and Arabic traditions. She has brilliantly subverted an often-repeated scholarly consensus that the Arabic and Syriac narratives had at some stage found their way into a Greek history, now lost, that was ascribed to a certain Theophilus of Edessa.[10] The Greek origin of the later Semitic narratives allows us to come very close to the events that Theophanes adapted for his Christian readers, and it reveals a scene in Jerusalem that is wholly consistent with the archaeological record for the Muslim advance into Palestine. That advance was peaceful and diplomatic. By straightening out the tangle of sources in Greek, Syriac, and Arabic Conterno has made a major advance in understanding what happened in Jerusalem in 638, only six years after the Prophet's death.

Once the Muslims had taken possession of Jerusalem, the general ʿAmr ibn al Āṣ took his forces out of Palestine into Egypt and succeeded in occupying Alexandria, despite an aborted Byzantine attempt later to recover it. He established the Muslim presence in Egypt at Fusṭaṭ, in the vicinity of southern Cairo near the former Byzantine garrison on the Nile at Egyptian Babylon. What happened in Egypt under ʿUmar was essentially an extension of the largely nonviolent occupation that characterized the moves into Syria and Palestine. Life went on more or less as it had been. Present evidence indicates that the use of papyri for preparing documents and contracts seems to have started in Egypt after the Muslims arrived, at least by 642, which is the earliest date for papyri after the occupation. Initially the language and script are Greek, but Arabic appears in a famous bilingual papyrus of the following year.[11] It is a receipt for sheep, and it is written in both Greek and Arabic in a milieu that, as a cross indicates, was clearly Christian. But the Christian Greek formula "in the name of God" is balanced in Arabic by the Islamic *bismillah,* "in the name of God, the merciful and compassionate." Both languages are competently written and imply previous documentary use in the region.

Perhaps the most startling feature of the bilingual papyrus of 643 is the word used to describe the invading people. They are called *magaritai,* which is a term that also occurs in Syriac as *mhagrayê.* These names are simply Greek and Syriac forms of the Arabic *muhājirūn,* who are the people who made the *hijra.* Since Muḥammad's Believers had made the *hijra* over twenty years before by going from Mecca to Medina, their name in their new territories shows that the word had lost its original meaning and served now to designate them simply as the incoming Arabs. Presumably this is because they referred to themselves in this way, and their new neighbors had taken over the name.

In 644 a disaffected slave stabbed 'Umar in Medina and thereby altered the interim administration that had been set up at the Prophet's death. As he was dying, 'Umar convoked a small advisory council *(shūra)* to determine who should succeed him, and the choice fell to an influential member of the Umayyads who had been married to two of Muḥammad's daughters, 'Uthmān ibn 'Affān. His emergence as the next caliph anticipated the dynasty of his clan, which was to take shape under Mu'āwiya in 661 at the end of the Medinan interregnum.

'Uthmān is best known as the caliph who attempted to create a canonical, or vulgate, text of the Qur'ān in order to impart a stable form to the word of God. The texts in use for recitation or reading were not always or everywhere the same, and this seemed, and still seems today, unacceptable imprecision in divine utterances. Uthmān's order to collect and compare extant texts was designed to create a definitive version in a limited number of copies (four to seven, according to various accounts), to be placed in designated urban centers, and it reflected a need within the new faith to have a sacred book about which there could be no question. But there was no way to eliminate earlier written copies, and palimpsests discovered in the Great Mosque of Ṣan'ā' have proven that texts before the Uthmanic vulgate were actually preserved. Consequently debate continues about the nature, or even the very existence, of the codices commissioned by 'Uthmān, and it is clear that a canonical text emerged only gradually.[12] The earliest documentary quotations from the Qur'ān appeared in 691 in the inscriptions in the Dome of the Rock in Jerusalem, and it has long been recognized that some parts of them are paraphrases of the canonical readings together with interpolations: "The Umayyad mosaic epigraphy [in the Dome of the Rock] contains selections from the Holy Koran interspersed with many pious phrases, supplications, and remarks on the original construction."[13] Whatever 'Uthmān did may have contributed to the creation of the Qur'ān as we have it today, but this neither wiped out earlier versions nor instantly established an invariable and canonical one.

'Uthmān's career was abruptly terminated by assassins in 656. They had made their way to his house in Medina from opposition groups both in Egypt at

Fusṭaṭ and in Iraq at Baṣra and Kūfa. The emergence of these dissidents from the west and east of the Muslim heartland seems to have been connected to the influence of the Quraysh and the growing resentment they aroused. Even the Prophet's widow, 'A'isha, departed on a pilgrimage as the opposition was boiling up. She was evidently disinclined to support the beleaguered caliph. His successor for four years more was the cousin and son-in-law of Muḥammad 'Alī ibn Abī Ṭālib, against whom 'A'isha is said to have nourished a long-standing grudge for questioning her virtue many years earlier. Although a cousin of the Prophet, he did not belong to the Quraysh but to the Hāshim, and the Quraysh profited from 'A'isha's enmity to 'Alī to express their disapproval of him by leaving Medina to join 'A'isha in Mecca, as did Marwān, the leader of 'Uthmān's Umayyads. 'Alī inherited in Damascus a powerful Umayyad governor of Syria, Mu'āwiya, who had been there for two decades and, though disinclined to come to his support, demanded that his kinsman's murder be avenged.

In the midst of this rapidly deteriorating situation 'Alī had to deal with increasingly militant opposition in Iraq. The balance of power in the movement that Muḥammad had launched in Mecca and Medina now shifted with his fourth successor to Baṣra and

Kūfa. 'A'isha herself made her way into the region along with 'Alī's enemies. He confronted them all in a battle outside Baṣra that is known, from the animal that was actually transporting 'A'isha, as the Battle of the Camel. Others came out—Kharijites, from the Arabic *kharaja* (go out)—to join the civil insurrection against the fourth caliph, who had by now installed himself in Kūfa. This moment marked the definitive end to the supremacy of Mecca and Medina as the Arabian centers of power for the heirs of Muḥammad. 'Alī failed to neutralize the machinations of Mu'āwiya in Damascus, and after a military engagement near Raqqa on the west bank of the Euphrates he was induced to enter into negotiations with Mu'āwiya's people at Udhruḥ, not far from Petra—in a diplomatic encounter that has been rightly characterized as a farce.[14] The poisoned saber that struck 'Alī in the forehead at Kūfa in January 661 came from a Kharijite and brought an end to what is considered the first Muslim civil war *(fitna)*. It allowed Mu'āwiya to secure his position in Damascus as the first caliph of the first Islamic dynasty, the Umayyads. But in death 'Alī became much more powerful than he had been while alive, and he remains today the supreme martyr of the influential break-away group

Muslims called simply the Shiʿa, which means a "sect" or "faction."

The era of the four caliphs who were designated in subsequent tradition as orthodox *(rāshidūn)* marked the irreversible transfer of the center of Islamic administration from Mecca and Medina, first to Damascus, and, in 750, with the Abbasids, to Baghdad. Perhaps the most remarkable feature of this era, which terminated in a brief civil war, was the almost imperceptible impact that it had upon the Byzantine culture of the region. The orthodox caliphs simply showed no interest, apart from imposing some taxes to pay for their soldiers and other routine costs, in imposing their own language, religion, or traditions upon the lands into which they had moved. Churches continued to function as before, and were treated as holy places. The Byzantine coinage remained in circulation, and administrative documents continued to be issued in Greek. Archaeological investigation, which has been cultivated for this period in recent years, confirms the lack of any substantial impact of the Muslims on local populations.[15]

8

A NEW DISPENSATION

The first caliph of the new Umayyad dynasty, Mu'āwiya, had long served as governor in Damascus for the interregnum of the *rāshidūn* after Muḥammad's death. His decision to remain in Damascus after succeeding 'Alī was portentous, because it meant that the administration of the Islamic Empire would not return to its origins in Mecca or Medina. Mecca and its *ḥaram* preserved the sanctity with which the ancient Ka'ba and the Prophet, who had reconstructed the Ka'ba, endowed it. But from 661 onward, down to the present time, the administrative centers of Islam were to lie outside Arabia, with the seven-year exception of the civil war *(fitna)* led by ibn al-Zubayr from Mecca and Medina against the succession of 'Abd al-Malik in 685. Mu'āwiya had inherited in Syria, Palestine, Iraq, and Egypt a vast part of the Near East that had formerly belonged to the Byzantine or Persian Empires. But when he assumed the caliphate in 661 the Persian Empire of the Sassanians had already been overthrown, and the Byzantine Empire, which was widely known as the second Rome, or simply as Rome, was still centered in Byzantium, though by now reduced in the east to Asia Minor and Cyprus. The city had officially taken the name of Constantinople from the founder of its empire, and that is the name that has survived among Hellenophones to this day. Its western territories in northern Greece and Macedonia were constantly under threat from westward migrations coming from the east by way of the Caucasus and westward above the Black Sea. The situation for Byzantium—the second Rome—was inherently unstable, and Muʿāwiya knew it. This instability lasted until it finally fell before the Ottoman Turks in 1453, and a third Rome arose in Moscow.[1]

Muʿāwiya's principal objective as the first Umayyad caliph was to take Constantinople and extend his power across Asia Minor, thereby consolidating the Persian and Byzantine realms into a single Muslim Empire. This was a strategy that he had already tried to implement by attacking Cyprus from the sea, even when he was still governor in Damascus. After becoming caliph he continued to challenge the Byzantines with ships in addition to sending troops overland as far as Chalcedon. He laid siege to Constantinople but was ultimately repulsed by the

Byzantines, who now had at their disposal the terrifying and devastating weapon known as "Greek Fire." Mu'āwiya's obsession with adding the last great component of the Byzantine Empire to his own meant that he was too preoccupied to do anything of consequence to alter the rhythm of life in the Near Eastern lands that he already ruled.

As we have observed, it has only recently become clear from examination of the archaeological record that in Palestine, Syria, and Transjordan hardly anything changed in the patterns of daily life, including religion and cultivation of the land, from the beginning of the Muslim invasions right through to the end of the caliphate of Mu'āwiya.[2] Older and traditional modern accounts too readily accepted the triumphalist narratives promulgated by the later Arab historians, while the overly dramatic accounts of Christian chronographers such as Theophanes Confessor in the ninth century, and others after him, deliberately recast and reinterpreted what they found in sources from the seventh and eighth centuries.[3] The only surviving historical text of any length from the late seventh century, the narrative of the Armenian Sebeos (who was writing at a time when the ships of Mu'āwiya were approaching the shores of Constantinople), provides no warrant for assuming major social or administrative changes in the Near East during the tumultuous events that brought down the Persian Empire. Sebeos was greatly interested in these events and was aware that some peoples were uprooted, such as the Jews in Edessa. He even knew that these Jews on occasion threw in their lot with the Arabs, but this was not an arrangement that lasted for long.[4]

Reports of the seven-year Arab siege of Caesarea on the coast of Palestine in the middle of the seventh century may conceivably be accurate about the duration of the siege, but they find almost no confirmation in the archaeological record. That siege, despite its length, seems to have passed without much violence in the city, and other major cities, such as Jerusalem, Scythopolis (Bet She'an), and Gerasa show a comparable lack of violence or destruction throughout the seventh century after the arrival of the Arabs. The invaders seemed glad to have found a society in place that had been functioning well enough under the Byzantines, and offered a tolerance that threatened none of the various faiths and sacred places in the region. The Arabs were obviously disinclined to disrupt the equilibrium of the status quo.

The invaders show every sign of having adopted the social organization that they found, and this included leaving churches in place, or even using them to worship with their fellow monotheists. It included the use of Greek in commercial transactions, as reflected in the papyri, and the widespread circulation and imitation of coinage that had been introduced by the Byzantines.[5] The mints at which the so-called Arab-Byzantine coins were struck remain largely unidentified, and it was not until the later seventh century that the first of the bilingual Arab coinage, with legends in Arabic as well as Greek, began to appear. The slow and late emergence of Arabic under Muʿāwiya is another reflection of Muslim acceptance of the society that passed under Arab control. It was only the collapse of the government in Damascus after Muʿāwiya's death that precipitated administrative and social changes, and that was at the cost of a second civil war *(fitna)*, which revived the fierce enmities of the first. That had been the war in which Muʿāwiya ultimately succeeded ʿAlī to inaugurate the dynasty of the Umayyads.

When Muʿāwiya died in 680, he had designated his son Yazid as the next caliph, but after little more than three years Yazid himself died and was succeeded by another Umayyad, Marwān ibn al-Ḥakam, whose accession provided the opportunity for an older and respected member of the Quraysh, ʿAbdallah ibn al-Zubayr, to lay claim to the caliphate. This was a man who had actually known the Prophet and served as one of his companions, and he was, like Muḥammad, a Qurashi. Emblematically he chose to establish himself in Mecca, where he could not only make a connection with the founder of Islam but assume control over the pilgrimages to the sacred space that enclosed the Kaʿba. Hence when Marwān soon died, his son and designated successor, ʿAbd al-Malik, found himself confronted with a counter-caliph in the person of ibn al-Zubayr, whose legitimacy, though denied in the subsequent Muslim tradition, was widely acknowledged at the time.[6]

This second civil war of early Islam left enduring scars through the proliferation of a rebel sect known as Kharijites, who had broken away (literally, "gone out") from the supporters of ʿAlī and maintained a pious, not to say sanctimonious, lifestyle of devotion to the Qur'ān that put them at odds with the Umayyad caliphate in Damascus as well as with the devotees of ʿAlī. They had foresworn ʿAlī's party *(shiʿa),* which we have seen became known simply as the Shiʿa. This occurred at the same time as the supporters of Muʿāwiya, who had been opposed to ʿAlī and his Shiʿa, claimed, for their part, to be the faithful custodians of the Muslim practice *(sunna)* of the Prophet. They therefore identified themselves as Sunni, who thereby set themselves up as another influential faction spawned by the revolt of the Kharijites. This meant that the second civil war, whose factions had taken their origins in the struggles of the first, had by now laid down the lineaments of hostilities in Islam that would have a long and disruptive future before them—the mutually irreconcilable sects of Shi'a and Sunni.

But 'Abd al-Malik proved to be an uncommonly astute caliph, once the struggle with ibn al-Zubayr and the short-lived revival of Mecca as a capital were finally terminated in 691. Ibn al-Zubayr was the first ruler to bring substantial and productive change to the administrative system that his predecessors had been content to take over from the Byzantines with scarcely any alteration throughout the territories that the Muslim armies had acquired. With 'Abd al-Malik the Umayyads finally established Arabic as the official language of administration, and they launched an imperial coinage that replaced the residual Arab-Byzantine coinage that been used for decades before him. He initially issued bronze, silver, and gold coins from some eighteen mints spread across his empire, from southeast Turkey through Syria and Palestine. These issues bear not only his name but a standing portrait, which has led numismatists to refer to them as "Standing Caliph" coins.[7] But 'Abd al-Malik subsequently removed all images from the coinage and made aniconic issues henceforth the standard for Islamic states.[8] The Islamic administration that had so long been in flux from Muḥammad's time through the orthodox caliphs and during two civil wars at last acquired its definitive shape under 'Abd al-Malik. This was the ultimate legacy of Mu'āwiya's success in anchoring the Umayyad regime in Damascus. The long and turbulent era of transition from Byzantium to Islam finally achieved stability through the energetic and visionary caliph at the end of the seventh century, but only after the challenge of ibn al-Zubayr had come to an end.

The visual proof of his achievement arose in Jerusalem on the former Temple site, known as the Ḥaram al-sharīf, where 'Abd al-Malik caused the magnificent Dome of the Rock to be constructed in 691–692. The date is secure, even though a later ruler inserted his own name in place of 'Abd al-Malik's on the building. But what remains unclear to this day is whether the date indicates the completion of the building, as might be expected, or the time at which construction was started. In view of the conclusion of the struggle with ibn al-Zubayr at that time it might seem more plausible to connect the launching of this great enterprise with the emergence of ʿAbd al-Malik as the uncontested caliph. Yet it is by no means inconceivable that he initiated the project in the last years of his war with the regime in Mecca as a visible assertion of his authority in the region. ʿAbd al-Malik's elimination of the cross on coin types he inherited from the Byzantines, together with his move to aniconic design and his imposition of Arabic as the language of his empire, proclaim the direction in which he was leading the Umayyad government. Greek had long been the primary language of the Christians, after the Aramaic of Jesus and his first Jewish followers. But over time Christians had come to proclaim their faith in many other Near Eastern tongues, including Armenian, Ethiopic, Syriac, and eventually Arabic itself. But in the momentous transition that occurred at the end of the seventh century the imposition of Arabic as the language of empire represented a decisive affirmation of the Islamic victory over Byzantium in the caliphate.

When the Prophet emigrated to Yathrib and renamed it as Medina, the city *(medina)* of Islam, this had been a decisive step in consolidating the new faith. From that moment onward, Mecca, which had acquired its blazing but short-lived prominence from the presence of Muḥammad, quickly receded into the fabric of other Arabian cities and shrines. Abortive efforts to re-establish its authority as a capital city of Islam in the middle of the seventh century, during the waning days of the so-called orthodox caliphs *(rāshidūn),* had utterly failed, as had the claims of ibn al-Zubayr, and Mecca returned once again to what it had been in the beginning, a sacred precinct for pilgrims. Along with constructing the Dome of the Rock, ʿAbd al-Malik reportedly attended to renovation of the Kaʿba by repeating and extending the rebuilding and cleansing that Muḥammad himself had initiated.[9] With the Umayyads securely based in Damascus, and after them the Abbasids in Baghdad, Mecca became the point of orientation for prayers and the destination of the *hajj,* but it was never again to be the center of Islamic administration.

No bureaucrat, no matter how astute, could have orchestrated a more flexible structure for the future of Islam than the separation of caliphate and *ḥaram.* As the central shrine of the faithful, Mecca brought Muslims together to worship, but it also allowed for an immense and perilous diversity in the formation of their sects and their states. What might have happened if the Umayyads had ruled from Mecca is one of the great imponderables of history.

9

THE DOME OF THE ROCK

THE GLEAMING DOME of the great Umayyad mosque that we know as the Dome of the Rock arose in 691–692, according to the mosaic inscription it bears, and it was therefore the work of ʿAbd al-Malik. Even though a rivalrous Abbasid caliph in the ninth century put his own name in place of that of ʿAbd al-Malik, there is universal agreement that this is indeed his building. What remains unclear is whether the date on the inscription indicates the beginning of work on the building or the completion of it, and this uncertainty is never likely to go away. As we have seen, this great undertaking either reflected the last years of ʿAbd al-Malik's struggle with ibn al-Zubayr, or it was launched at the end of it. But in either case it has dominated the city of Jerusalem from that time until this.

The dome, which radiates a golden glow from miles away, is actually constructed from wood covered with a gilded aluminum alloy, and it sits atop a cylindrical

Dome of the Rock, Jerusalem. Andriy Kravchenko / Alamy.

base that stands over a huge exposed rock around which circle the upper and lower ambulatories of a surrounding octagonal wall. These ambulatories allow contemplation of a series of grandly calligraphed Arabic texts in the arcades. They appear to incorporate excerpts, or perhaps echoes, of the Qur'ān as we have it. The entire building, once it was built, proclaimed the achievement of ʻAbd al-Malik in overcoming resistance to his rule in the civil war *(fitna)* that ibn al-Zubayr launched from Mecca. It secured Jerusalem definitively as one of the greatest holy places of Islam in addition to Mecca and Medina. Through its visibility and prominence it constitutes perhaps the single closest link between the early Umayyad caliphate and the present day. The octagon of the Dome of the Rock and the black cube of the Kaʻba stand together as the two holiest and most recognizable monuments of the contemporary Muslim world.

The Dome of the Rock is located in Jerusalem upon what had been known as Mount Moriah. This mount is believed to have served as the site of Solomon's Temple, which was destroyed in 587–586 BC when the Assyrians took the Jews of Jerusalem into captivity in Babylon. It was certainly the site of the temple that succeeded Solomon's, the so-called Second Temple,

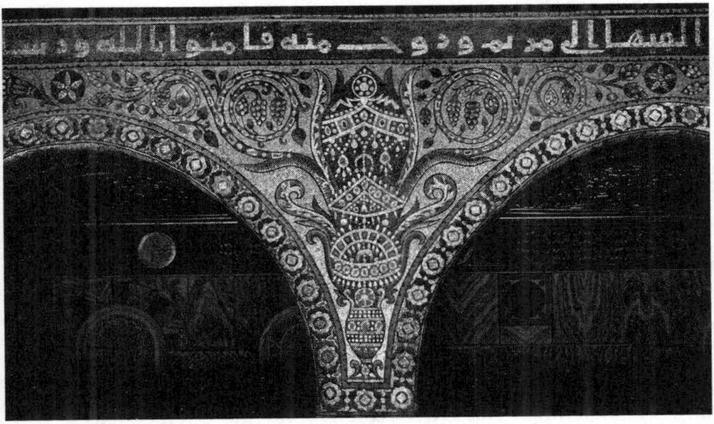

Spandrel from octagonal arcade, inner face of east side, Dome of the Rock, courtesy of Said Nuseibeh.

which was built after the Babylonian captivity of the Jews. This holy place consisted of a trapezoidal stone platform on the surface of the mount. Little is known about the Second Temple in its Hellenistic phase because Herod the Great undertook to overhaul completely the Second Temple building as he found it. What he left behind was the structure that Titus and Vespasian brought down in their war against the Jews in AD 70. Vestiges of it, including the present Wailing Wall, remain sacred for all Jews today. The mount itself, often called the Temple Mount in English, is known in Arabic as the Ḥaram al sharīf, "the Noble Sanctuary." 'Abd al-Malik erected his Dome of the Rock upon a small trapezoidal platform that was itself constructed upon the esplanade that may have originally constituted the stone platform for the Solomonic mount.

The whole complex lies in the southeastern corner of the walled city of Jerusalem, but because of its elevation and its radiance the Dome shines brightly in any view of the city from the surrounding territories, including Mount Zion, the Mount of Olives, and Golgotha. The continuity from the late seventh century to the third millennium of our era is as miraculous as the building itself.[1]

After 'Umar introduced Islam to Jerusalem in 638, with the cooperation of the patriarch Sophronius, a half-century was to elapse before the Umayyads were finally able to bring a systematic administrative structure to the city and to the whole region. We have observed earlier that it was only late in this period of transition that the entrenched Greek language and culture of Byzantine Palestine were finally supplanted by a bureaucracy conducted in Arabic and a coinage that reflected the faith of its rulers. The Dome of the Rock was the culmination of this slow and, for long periods, remarkably peaceful process of change. It was a process that was far less disruptive or violent for the local populations than it sometimes was for the Muslims themselves as rival parties struggled for control. One must therefore ask what stood on the Ḥaram al sharīf between 'Umar's arrival in Jerusalem and the accession of 'Abd al-Malik. This was a period of some four curiously unproductive decades of Umayyad rule, in the course of which two civil wars came and went. Fortunately, and surprisingly, we have an answer from an unexpected source.

In about 680 a Frankish bishop called Arculf is reported to have visited Palestine. All that we know about this otherwise unknown bishop appears in a work on holy places, *De Locis Sanctis,* written by Adomnán, the abbot of the Irish monastery at Iona in Scotland. According to Adomnán, Arculf was shipwrecked somewhere along the coast, after which he had extensive conversations, either at Iona or conceivably elsewhere, in which he related to Adomnán the details of his Near Eastern travels. This narration sufficiently impressed the abbot to write down Arculf's travelogue for future generations. Adomnán's Latin text not only survives for us to read today but was already available, not long after it was written, to the Venerable Bede, who made excerpts from it.[2]

It has become clear in recent years that parts of the *De Locis Sanctis* reflect written texts that might have been available at Iona, above all Jerome's register of holy places in Palestine, and that the abbot might have been more interested in exegetical problems involving biblical places than in a travelogue.[3] Since the very name Arculf is unique, the existence of the bishop himself has been called into question. But after an onslaught of revisionist skepticism, a consensus has finally emerged that Adomnán's work contains much eyewitness evidence that simply could not otherwise have been accessible to him at Iona. He may be assumed, reasonably enough, to have incorporated in the narration he heard from the Frankish bishop other material to which he might have had access. But this still leaves a precious residue of eyewitness testimony from a visitor to Palestine in the late seventh century. Robert Hoyland and Sarah Waidler have emphasized this point in a recent contribution, which argues decisively that historians have no warrant to write off Adomnán and Arculf's travels as fiction.[4]

Near the beginning of his account of Jerusalem, Arculf explicitly refers to what he observed in the space of the Ḥaram: "In the celebrated place where once the temple arose in its magnificence, situated towards the east near the wall, the Saracens now have a quadrangular prayer house [*quadrangulam orationis domum*]. They built it in a crude fashion with upright boards and large wooden beams over some ruined remains. The house can hold, it is said, three thousand people."

This precious testimony provides a unique glimpse of the Ḥaram just a little over a decade before the Dome of the Rock. It is as valuable for what it does not mention as for what it does. There was clearly a large mosque of simple wooden construction on the site. Such a building consecrated to prayer leaves no doubt about the sanctity of the place for a large number of Muslims, who must have included pilgrims as well as residents. But, more significantly, Arculf says nothing about the huge rock over which the Dome was subsequently built, and we must assume either that the mosque to which Arculf referred was built over it or, if the rock was exposed, that he simply did not see it.

In view of the prominence of the rock and its association with Muḥammad's night journey *(isrā')* from Mecca to Jerusalem, which is celebrated in Sura 17 of the Qur'ān, it would be far easier to believe that the quadrangular wooden mosque for 3,000 people was actually situated over and around the rock. If it had been exposed in the mosque, it would be hard to believe that Arculf could have missed it or failed to mention it. In the words of Sura 17:1 in the Qur'ān, "Glory to the Him Who took His servant [Muḥammad] for a journey by night from the Mosque of the Ḥaram [in Mecca] to the Farthest Mosque (*masjid al-aqsā* [in Jerusalem]), whose precincts We [God] have blessed, so that We could show him [Muḥammad] some of Our signs, for he is the hearer and the seer."[5]

Later Muslim tradition adorned the night journey with details of the Prophet's arrival in Jerusalem at the Bāb al-nabī, or Prophet's Gate, which is believed to be the double gate under the present al-Aqsa Mosque that is situated on the mount opposite the Dome of the Rock. The archangel Gabriel is reported to have met Muḥammad there. The two prayed together near the Rock, after which the winged horse Burāq conveyed the Prophet into the heavens. The Rock tried to rise up to follow him, but either Gabriel or Muḥammad himself held it back. All the prophets who had preceded Muḥammad then rose to greet him to acknowledge that he was the last and the greatest of many prophets. He was then vouchsafed a vision of hell and paradise, with their attendant terrors and joys. The aborted attempt of the Rock to rise from the ground explains, according to tradition, the cave that now exists beneath it as well as the mysterious marks on its surface that were thought to have been made by the foot and hand of God Himself at the time of the Creation.[6] This remarkable interpretation was accepted in the seventh century, although Muslim orthodoxy later rejected it because it impiously implied a corporeal divinity.

Muslim tradition also associated the discovery of the Rock in the Ḥaram with Sophronius's introduction of 'Umar into Jerusalem in 638. It was said that when 'Umar declined Sophronius's proposal that he pray at the Church of the Holy Sepulchre, the two of them reportedly ascended to the Temple esplanade, which was then covered with ruins, and there 'Umar saw the Rock and decided to build a mosque.[7] If there is anything reliable in this story, it would seem that this was the moment at which the vast quadrangular mosque that Arculf saw was constructed, and that this new and capacious mosque encompassed the Rock from which Muḥammad rose up to view hell and paradise.

The construction of the Dome of the Rock at Jerusalem, whether a few years before 691 or in that year, was 'Abd al-Malik's direct response to the gradual and ultimately successful suppression of the rival government of ibn al-Zubayr in Mecca. As such it would have confirmed the prior sacrality of the Rock and its site. The wooden mosque that Arculf saw exemplified the sacred character of the place. In Arculf's day, as we have seen, a Muslim tradition was current, though subsequently discredited, that the marks on the Rock were impressions of the foot and hand of God Himself, the only traces of His presence on earth after the Creation. If ʿAbd al-Malik was aware of this interpretation of the marks—whatever and whenever the origin of the story, and we will never know whether he was—the sacrality of the Rock seems clearly to date from the earliest years of the Muslim occupation of Jerusalem. The glorious building erected over it at once became a powerful and enduring symbol of Islam and conferred upon Jerusalem a status that only Mecca could match.

Accordingly, because of its huge symbolic importance just as the Umayyad dynasty was consolidating its Arab administration in the region, it is reasonable to ask what kind of message ʿAbd al-Malik was sending out to the world by his construction of the Dome of the Rock. Fortunately he proclaimed his message in the series of magnificently calligraphed texts that he caused to be put on display in mosaic inscriptions along both the outer and the inner faces of the arcades of the two octagonal ambulatories. These texts include repetitions of the *bismillah* (in the name of Allāh), invoking God (Allāh) as compassionate and merciful as well as affirming him to be the one God with no other. But interwoven with all these assertions of God's uniqueness and mercy are phrases from the Qur'ān, largely but not entirely in the canonical form of this sacred text as it is recited today in what is believed to be the recension created by 'Uthmān.[8] Oleg Grabar has raised the interesting possibility that the divergences from the supposedly Uthmanic text may reflect an oral tradition that outlasted the establishment of the Holy Book in its canonical form. He has even speculated whether it is legitimate to speak of quotations from the Qur'ān, but he concluded by accepting the idea of quotation along with variants that arose through memory of an oral tradition.[9]

Whatever the precise explanation for the lines with Quranic material, the intentions of 'Abd al-Malik can best be inferred from the words that were chosen to be displayed so conspicuously along the inner and outer faces of the octagon. Grabar has interestingly evoked the replacement of images with writing on 'Abd al-Malik's gold and silver coins for comparison with the use of writing to convey a message in the Dome of the Rock.[10] If the caliph did indeed consider words the most potent means of conveying his aims, as the numismatic evidence would imply, it is likely that the octagonal inscriptions in his magnificent building were drafted with the greatest care. When the Abbasid caliph al-Ma'mūn in the ninth century put his name in place of that of 'Abd al-Malik's without so much as bothering to change the late seventh-century date, it is clear that what mattered, apart from self-aggrandizement, was the theological content of the inscriptions. Of course many of these simply reinforce what appears in the *bismillah,* and this is also true of Quranic material on the east and north doors.

But the texts from the Qur'ān on the inner octagonal face are much more noteworthy because they incorporate citations from the fourth and nineteenth suras of the Qur'ān that directly confront Christian traditions about Mary and Jesus. The first of these, from the fourth sura, may be rendered as follows:

> O people of the Book, do not go beyond the bounds of your religion and do not say about God anything but the truth. Indeed the Messiah Jesus, son of Mary, was a messenger of God and He bestowed His word upon her as well as His spirit. So believe in God and His messengers, and do not say "Three." Stop, it is better for

> you. For God is one God, He is too exalted to have a son. To Him belongs what is in heaven and on earth, and it is enough for Him to be a protector. The Messiah does not disdain to be a servant of God, nor do the angels nearest to Him. Those who disdain serving Him and who are arrogant—all these will God gather to Himself.

At this point the text makes a rapid transition, with the words "Bless Your messenger and Your servant Jesus, son of Mary," to lines that appear in the nineteenth sura. The Quranic text resumes with these words:

> Peace be upon him on the day of his birth and upon the day of his death and upon the day he is raised up alive.[11] This is Jesus, son of Mary. They dispute over a matter of truth: It is not for God to take a son. Glory be to Him, when He decrees something He only says "Be" and it is. God is indeed my Lord and your Lord.[12] Therefore serve Him. This is the straight path.

The inclusion of these two unambiguous texts about the origins and doctrines of early Christianity in so conspicuous a place among the inscriptions of the inner octagonal arcade can only have been deliberate. It must tell us something about the disposition of the caliph toward the faith of the Byzantine Empire that his own had ultimately supplanted in the city of the Christians' Holy Sepulchre. It was in the most ancient holy place in this city that he chose to build the Dome of the Rock. These texts explicitly recognize Jesus as a messenger from God, through His word and His spirit (or breath, *rūḥ*), given to Mary. Every Muslim knew that Muḥammad as Prophet was similarly a messenger of God, but the Quranic acknowledgment of Jesus as another divine messenger brings together the two great monotheist religions, Christianity and Islam. Yet this acknowledgment was not allowed to obscure the awkward fact that the Christian doctrine of the Trinity was a dissonant component in this conjunction of monotheisms. The texts in the Dome of the Rock clearly acknowledge the shared monotheism of both the new faith and the older one, but at the same time they firmly reject any notion of three-in-one.

This rejection, which is anchored in the Qur'ān, was securely rooted in the teachings of Muḥammad and in the revelations given to him by Gabriel. On the north door of the Dome of the Rock an inscription explicitly spells out Muḥammad's role in relation to other religions through a text that also derives from the Qur'ān, but in a verse that actually occurs twice, in two different suras.[13] Muḥammad is proclaimed to be God's messenger, "whom He sent with guidance and the religion of truth—to proclaim it over all religion, even though the polytheists [the *mushrikūn*, or sharers] hate it." It is clear that polytheism stood as the immovable obstacle in the Muslim embrace of other religions. To the extent that Christianity included what seemed to be a deviation from strict monotheism through its doctrine of the Trinity, it was partially polytheist and therefore abhorrent to Islam. But to the extent that Christianity was, at least in principle, also monotheist as well as a "religion of the book" it could find a place in Islam. By highlighting these issues, 'Abd al-Malik was both addressing and instructing the community of Believers on what his Muslim predecessors had quietly subsumed into their administration over the past half-century. It looks as if the caliph wanted to show the limits of Muslim toleration as he moved to transform a Christian and Byzantine administration into a Muslim and Arab one.

Nothing in the calligraphed texts suggests that 'Abd al-Malik had any interest in converting the Christians, but simply in showing that the orthodox doctrine of the Trinity was incompatible with absolute monotheism. This was of course an issue that had formerly engaged Christian theologians themselves. The Islamic Empire was home to many Monophysites or Miaphysites (believers in "one nature" of Christ), who had separated themselves from Byzantium after the Council of Chalcedon in 451 in a complex debate over Christ's nature. The parts of the old Byzantine Empire that espoused Monophysitism, above all greater Syria and Egypt, were now integral parts of the new Islamic Empire, and Ethiopia, which was a close neighbor, also supported Monophysite Christians. Although the Monophysites in the Islamic sphere of influence would naturally have believed in the Trinity, their militant espousal of one nature might have rendered them more sympathetic to a reader of the Qur'ān.

'Abd al-Malik chose knowingly to proclaim in Jerusalem his recognition of Jesus as a messenger of God and of Mary as the recipient of God's Word and Spirit. The reference to the Word *(kalām)* in the calligraphed text may even reflect acquaintance with the New Testament's *Logos,* as most famously seen at the opening of the Gospel of John, while the Spirit *(ruḥ)* appears to reproduce the Greek *pneuma.* But emphatically denying the Trinity can only be read as a comment upon the orthodoxy that was celebrated nearby in the Church of the Holy Sepulchre. It not only put these two great holy places into dialogue with each other, but it made them fundamentally incompatible. That did not augur well for the future, even if it recognized how much Islam and Christianity had in common.

What 'Abd al-Malik's Dome of the Rock conspicuously fails to address is the oldest monotheism in Jerusalem, the faith of the Jews. That is all the more remarkable because 'Abd al-Malik must certainly have been aware that he was building precisely where the Jews' Second Temple once had stood, to say nothing of the Temple of Solomon himself. But he would undoubtedly have known that the Persian Empire in the time of Muḥammad had followed a consistent policy of supporting the Jews both in Palestine and in Arabia, to serve as a counterbalance to the Byzantine Christians. Although the Persian Empire no longer existed in the days of 'Abd al-Malik, the animosity it spawned among the Arabs continued to exist, and the embers of the fires that burned in Jerusalem in 614 were still glowing. The reconciliation of 'Umar and Sophronius had done nothing to improve the position of the Jews when their ancestral city became holy to Muslims as well as to Christians.

It would take many centuries before Jews and Muslims would be able to discern and to discuss what their monotheisms had in common. What they shared was a lineage that went all the way back to Abraham. No one understood this better than Maimonides in the twelfth century, who was fluent in Arabic and Hebrew, and had direct experience of the fanatical Muslim regime of the Almohads in Spain. In his magisterial epistle addressed to the Jews of Yemen, Maimonides confronted directly the incompatibility of the three great monotheist faiths, and the problems for any one of them in surviving under the rule of another.[14] He understood what it was to be a Jew in a Muslim state, and what it was to be a Jew in a Christian one. At least Christians and Jews had the Bible in common, but the Qur'ān was sacred only to the Muslims. 'Abd al-Malik's Dome of the Rock arose on ground that was shared by the three great monotheisms, but it proclaimed only one of them and offered no path to coexistence with the other two.

If both Muslims and Jews rejected the Trinitarian doctrine of the Christians, and if the sacred book of the Jews was no less sacred to the Christians, none of that sufficed to bind all the descendants of Abraham together. Consequently we have still today to wrestle with the incompatibilities that ʿAbd al-Malik bequeathed to the world in Jerusalem when he built the Dome of the Rock upon the Temple Mount. The formation of the vessel that Muḥammad bequeathed to the world under the name of Islam took place in a crucible of incompatible doctrines and traditions, and so it should hardly be surprising to find that these incompatibilities have endured as long as Islam itself. The history of the relationships between Judaism, Christianity, and Islam is replete with profound reflections on these issues in the work of major thinkers in all three traditions. Even if the disjunctions and disagreements are bound to remain with us, we must count ourselves fortunate that we can at least observe and describe the volatile components from which Islam emerged.

NOTES

SELECT BIBLIOGRAPHY

ACKNOWLEDGMENTS

INDEX

NOTES

Prologue

1. Fred M. Donner, *Muhammad and the Believers* (Cambridge, MA: Harvard University Press, 2010); Robert G. Hoyland, *In God's Path: The Arab Conquests and the Creation of an Islamic Empire* (New York: Oxford University Press, 2015); Aziz al-Azmeh, *The Emergence of Islam in Late Antiquity: Allāh and His People* (Cambridge: Cambridge University Press, 2014).
2. I do not propose to examine the possibility that Muḥammad died later than 632, despite Stephen J. Shoemaker, *The Death of a Prophet: The End of Muhammad's Life and the Beginnings of Islam* (Philadelphia: University of Pennsylvania Press, 2012). Two scrappy texts that make reference to him in 634, one in Greek and one in Syriac, scarcely warrant overturning one of the few securely anchored dates in the Islamic tradition.
3. Maria Conterno, *La "Descrizione dei tempi" all'alba dell'espansione islamica. Un'indagine sulla storiografia*

greca siriaca e araba fra VII e VIII secolo, Millennium Studies 47 (De Gruyter: Berlin, 2014).

4. Behnam Sadeghi and Mohsen Goudarzi, "Ṣanʿāʾ 1 and the Origins of Islam," *Der Islam* 87 (2010): 1–129.
5. Questions such as these have enlivened my years with two deeply missed colleagues at the Institute for Advanced Study in Princeton, Oleg Grabar and Patricia Crone, whose willingness to challenge orthodoxies was always supported by exceptional mastery of the sources, both visual and textual. I am deeply indebted to both of them and would like to honor their memory here. It is a sign of their openness that they often disagreed with one another, and I had occasion often to disagree with both of them—to my immense profit and, I hope, to the benefit of the present work. May the next generation be as fortunate in having such colleagues.

1. The Arabian Kingdom of Abraha

1. F. Villeneuve, C. Phillips, and W. Facey, "Une inscription latine de l'archipel Farasân (sud de la mer Rouge) et son contexte archéologique et historique," *Arabia: Revue de Sabéologie* 2 (2004): 143–190 with figs. 63–67. Also F. Villeneuve, "Une inscription latine sur l'archipel Farasân, Arabie Séoudite, sud de la mer Rouge," *CRAI* (2004): 419–429. For a discussion of the time when this

garrison was set up, see G. W. Bowersock, "Elio Aristide tra Atene e Roma," in *Elio Aristide e la legittimazione greca dell' impero di Roma* (Bologna: Il Mulino, 2013), 25–38, esp. 36.

2. A. R. Al-Ansary, *Qaryat al-Fau: A Portrait of Pre-Islamic Civilization in Saudi Arabia* (Riyadh and New York: University of Riyadh and St. Martin's Press, 1982); Christian Julien Robin, "Le Royaume Ḥujride, dit 'royaume de Kinda,' entre Ḥimyar et Byzance," *CRAI* (1996): 665–714.
3. G. W. Bowersock, *The Throne of Adulis* (New York: Oxford University Press, 2013), 78–91; C. J. Robin, "The Peoples beyond the Arabian Frontier in Late Antiquity: Recent Epigraphic Discoveries and Latest Advances," in *Inside and Out: Interactions between Rome and the Peoples on the Arabian and Egyptian Frontiers in Late Antiquity,* ed. J. H. F. Dijkstra and G. Fisher (Leuven: Peeters, 2014), 33–79, esp. 36–49.
4. Bowersock, *Throne of Adulis,* 63–77.
5. D. Genequand and C. J. Robin, eds., *Les Jafnides: Des rois arabes au service de Byzance* (Paris: De Boccard, 2015). For the Ghassānids, see, in this same volume, C. J. Robin, "Ghassān en Arabie," 79–120. On the Naṣrids, see now the thorough study by Isabel Toral-Niehoff, *Al-Ḥīra: Eine arabische Kulturmetropole im spätantiken Kontext* (Leiden:

Brill, 2014), which finally replaces G. Rothstein, *Die Dynastie der Laḫmiden in al-Ḥīra: Ein Versuch zur arabisch-persischen Geschichte zur Zeit der Sasaniden* (Berlin: Reuther & Reichard, 1899).

6. Richard E. Payne, *A State of Mixture: Christians, Zoroastrians, and Iranian Political Culture in Late Antiquity* (Oakland: University of California Press, 2015), explores this interaction in the late antique Sassanian territories.
7. For Joseph, see C. J. Robin, "Joseph, dernier roi de Ḥimyar," *Jerusalem Studies in Arabic and Islam* 34 (2008): 1–124. For Kālēb, see the Axumite inscription that appears as illustration no. 3, written in classical Ethiopic (Geʿez), from left to right, but in Sabaic script, with a clearly visible Christian cross at the beginning of the top line. On the details of Kālēb's expedition, see Bowersock, *Throne of Adulis,* 92–105.
8. Procop., *Bell. Pers.* 1. 20. 4.
9. For these events, see Bowersock, *Throne of Adulis,* 92–119.
10. Iwona Gajda, *Le royaume de Ḥimyar à l'époque monothéiste* (Paris: Académie des Inscriptions et Belles-Lettres, 2009), 118–121 ["Noms et titres d'Abraha"]. See also C. J. Robin, "Abraha's Reign: The Current State of Research," in Dijkstra and Fisher, *Inside and Out,* 65–71.
11. Procop., *Bell. Pers.* 1. 20. 4.

12. C. J. Robin, "La Grande Église d'Abraha à Ṣanʿāʾ: Quelques remarques sur son emplacement, ses dimensions et sa date," in *Interrelations between the Peoples of the Near East and Byzantium in Pre-Islamic Times,* ed. Vassilios Christides, vol. 3 of *Semitica Antiqua* (Córdoba: CNERU, 2015), 105–129.
13. CIS IV / CIH 541, most recently in W. W. Müller, *Sabäische Inschriften nach Ären datiert. Bibliographie, Texte und Glossar* (Wiesbaden: Harrassowitz, 2010), 110–117.
14. Theophylact Simocatta, *Hist.* 4. 11. 2–3.
15. For details, see Gajda, *Le royaume de Ḥimyar,* 123–126, and see 124 for comparison with the Church of the Nativity in Bethlehem and the Church of the Holy Sepulchre in Jerusalem.
16. See the annotations to al-Ṭabarī's account in the still invaluable translation by Theodor Nöldeke, *Die Geschichte der Perser und Araber zur Zeit der Sasaniden* (Leiden: Brill, 1879), 201–202.
17. See Müller, *Sabäische Inschriften,* 110–117; and also the discussion in Gajda, *Le royaume de Ḥimyar,* 126–130.
18. For the first of three Bi'r Muraygh̄an inscriptions, see Müller, *Sabäische Inschriften,* 118–119. For the most recent, see Gajda, *Le royaume de Ḥimyar,* 141.
19. See Gajda, *Le royaume de Ḥimyar,* 141 for verses of al-Mukhabbal al-Saʿdī on help furnished to Abraha during the battle of Ḥalibān.

20. C. J. Robin and S. Ṭayrān, "Soixante-dix ans avant l'Islam: l'Arabie toute entière dominée par un roi chrétien," *CRAI* (2012): 525–553. See also Robin, "The Peoples beyond the Arabian Frontier," 68–71.
21. See Nöldeke's analysis of this story in *Die Geschichte der Perser,* 220–221n4.
22. Paul Yule, "A Late Antique Christian King from Ẓafār, Southern Arabia," *Antiquity* 87 (2013): 1124–1135.
23. Paul Yule, ed., *Late Antique Arabia: Ẓafār, Capital of Ḥimyar, Rehabilitation of a 'Decadent' Society, Excavations of the Ruprecht-Karls-Universität Heidelberg 1998–2010 in the Highlands of the Yemen,* vol. 29 of Abhandlungen Deutsche Orient-Gesellschaft (Wiesbaden, 2013).
24. Gianfranco Fiaccadori, "Gregentios in the Land of the Homerites," in *Life and Works of Saint Gregentios, Archbishop of Taphar,* ed. Albrecht Berger (Berlin: de Gruyter, 2006), 54–55.

2. *Arab Paganism in Late Antiquity*

1. For late antique Ḥimyar and its history, see G. W. Bowersock, *The Throne of Adulis* (New York: Oxford University Press, 2013). On Ẓafār, see Chapter 1 in this volume and notes 23 and 24. On Yathrib, see Michael Lecker, "Were the Ghassānds and the Byzantines behind Muḥammad's *hijra?,*" in *Les Jafnides. Des rois arabes au service de Byzance,* ed.

D. Genequand and C. J. Robin, *Orient et Méditerranée* 17 (Paris: De Boccard, 2015), 277–293.

2. Toufic Fahd, *Le Panthéon de l'Arabie centrale à la veille de l'hégire* (Paris: P. Geuthner, 1968).
3. Ibn al-Kalbī, *Kitāb al aṣnām, or A Book of Idols: A History of Arab Worship before the Advent of Islam*, trans. Mohammad Reza Jalali Naini (Tehran: Taban Press, 1970).
4. Ishay Rosen-Zvi, "Paul and the Invention of the Gentiles," *Jewish Quarterly Review* 105 (2015): 1–41. This thorough and important analysis might have been clearer if the author had avoided discussing the issue by reference to the English "Gentile," which obviously Paul did not use. Rosen-Zvi rightly highlights the sense of *ethnos* in relation to *goy*, but Paul's *ethnê*, which included barbarians (Rom. 1:14), can be more inclusive than Gentile. Paul sometimes conveys the idea of Gentile by *hellēn* (Greek), as in Romans 1:16, 2:9, and 2:10.
5. See Gregory of Nazianzus's indignation over Julian's appropriation of Greek learning in *Orat.* 4: A. Kurmann, *Gregor von Nazianz, Oratio 4 gegen Julian, Ein Kommentar* (Basel: Reinhardt, 1988).
6. Pagan monotheism owes its prominence in current scholarship to the publication of *Pagan Monotheism in Late Antiquity*, ed. P. Athanassiadi and M. Frede (Oxford: Clarendon Press, 1999). For pre-Islamic Arab paganism, see G. R. Hawting, *The*

Idea of Idolatry and the Emergence of Islam (Cambridge: Cambridge University Press, 1999); and P. Crone, "The Religion of the Qur'ānic Pagans: God and the Lesser Deities," *Arabica* 57 (2010): 151–200.

7. Louis Robert, "Un oracle gravé à Oenoanda," *CRAI* (1971): 597–619, reprinted in *Opera Minora Selecta* (Amsterdam: Hakkert, 1989), 5:617–639.
8. Herod. 1.131 and 3.8.
9. For the marble statue of Allāt at Palmyra, see A. Sartre-Fauriat and M. Sartre, *Palmyre: La cité des caravanes* (Paris: Gallimard, 2008), 75. For the two images at Qaryat al-Fāw, see G. W. Bowersock, *Hellenism in Late Antiquity* (Ann Arbor: University of Michigan Press, 1990), plates 12 and 14.
10. See the extraordinary relief from the Ṣan'ā' national museum recently published by C. J. Robin in *Dieux et déesses d'Arabie* (Paris: De Boccard, 2012), 75. The angel is qualified as "very high" *('lyt)* and carries a rope, which designates destiny or fate.
11. For Arabian goddesses and angels, see G. W. Bowersock, "Les anges païens de l'antiquité tardive," *Cahiers Glotz* 24 (2013): 91–104, esp. 99–100.
12. The inscriptions are duly listed by J. Cantineau, s.v. MNWTW, in *Le Nabatéen* (Paris: Leroux, 1932), 2:116.
13. See now the thorough investigation by Al. Makin, *Representing the Enemy: Musaylima in Muslim Literature* (Frankfurt: Peter Lang, 2010).

14. Aziz al-Azmeh, "Arabian Monolatry and Ambient Monotheism," in his *The Emergence of Islam in Late Antiquity* (Cambridge: Cambridge University Press, 2014), 248–259.
15. M. Tardieu, "Ṣâbiens coraniques et 'ṣābiens' de Ḥarrān," *Journal asiatique* 274 (1986) : 1–44. See now Ilsetraut Hadot, *Le néoplatonicien Simplicius à la lumière des recherches contemporaines* (Sankt Augustin: Akademia, 2014), 53–80.
16. Uri Rubin, "Ḥanīfiyya and Ka'ba," *Jerusalem Studies in Arabic and Islam* 13 (1990): 85–112.
17. al-Azmeh, *The Emergence of Islam*, 363–365.
18. Bowersock, "Les anges païens de l'antiquité tardive."
19. P.-L. Gatier, "Inscriptions religieuses de Gérasa," *ADAJ* 26 (1982): 269.
20. Qur'ān 6:50 and 11:31.

3. Late Antique Mecca

1. The occupation of Mecca seems to have been at the initiative of Quṣayy, as told in Ibn Isḥāq's *Sira* 79–80. See A. Guillaume, *The Life of Muhammad* (Oxford: Oxford University Press, 1982), 52. For a skeptical view about Mecca as a cultic or commercial center before Quṣāyy, see Patricia Crone, *Meccan Trade and the Rise of Islam* (Princeton, NJ: Princeton University Press, 1987), 168.

2. M. Bukharin, "Mecca on the Caravan Routes in Pre-Islamic Antiquity," in *The Qur'ān in Context,* ed. A. Neuwirth et al. (Leiden: Brill, 2010), 115–134.
3. Crone, *Meccan Trade,* 187–190. The view of J. Wellhausen, *Reste arabischen Heidentums gesammelt und erläutet* (Berlin: Georg Reimer, 1887), that Hubal and Allāh were the same god under two successive names, is countered by the different functions of the gods. See C. J. Robin in *Oxford Handbook of Late Antiquity* (New York: Oxford University Press, 2012), 304.
4. J. Starcky and F. Zayadine, in the catalogue of the Museum of Lyon for the exhibition of 1978–1979, *Pétra et la Nabatène* (Muséum de Lyon: Lyon, 1978), 42–43.
5. P. C. Hammond, "Ein nabatäisches Weiherelief aus Petra," *Bonner Jahrbücher* 180 (1980): 265–269.
6. Robin, *Oxford Handbook of Late Antiquity,* 304.
7. Qur'ān 6:92 and 42:7.
8. H. Lammens, "La république marchande de la Mecque vers l'an 600 de notre ère," *Bulletin de l'Institut Égyptien* 4 (1910): 23–54.
9. Crone with critique by R. Serjeant, *JAOS* 110 (1990): 472–528 (see esp. 472, "a diatribe"); and Crone's reply in *Arabica* 39 (1992): 216–240.
10. See Bukharin, "Mecca on the Caravan Routes."
11. See Chapter 4 in this volume.

12. W. Montgomery Watt, *Muhammad at Mecca* (Oxford: Oxford University Press, 1953).
13. Crone, *Meccan Trade,* 134–136. But see Ptolemy, *Geog.* 6. 7.32, best consulted in *Klaudios Ptolemaios, Handbuch der Geographie,* ed. A. Stückelberger and G. Graßhoff (Basel: Schwabe, 2006), 2:630, with map on 874–875.
14. Crone, *Meccan Trade,* 136, seemed to expect the name of the city to be in Arabic, despite the absence of Arabic toponyms in this period.
15. Amm. Marcell. 23.6.47. Baraba is unknown, but may represent a deformation of Maraba for Marib.
16. Ptolemy shows a city called Gaia north of Hegra (Madā'in Ṣāliḥ), which is glossed as a polis, just as still greater cities are glossed as a metropolis. The word "polis" was not part of Gaia's name, as it clearly is in Ammianus's Geapolis / Hierapolis.
17. Mikhail Piotrovsky, "Koranicheskaya Archeologiya," in *Issledovaniya po Aravii i Islamu,* ed. A. V. Sedov (Moscow: Ministry of Culture of the Russian Federation, 2014).
18. For a heterodox view of these reports, in a polemic against Serjeant's reasonable espousal of the tradition, which is followed here, see Crone in *Arabica,* 221–223.
19. Bukharin, "Mecca on the Caravan Routes."
20. As is well shown by Richard E. Payne, *A State of Mixture: Christians, Zoroastrians, and Iranian Political*

Culture in Late Antiquity (Oakland: University of California Press, 2015).

21. This topic has been explored in an interesting, though eccentric, article by Jaakko Hämeen-Antilla, "Arabian Prophecy," in *Prophecy in Its Near Eastern Context: Mesopotamian, Biblical, and Arabian Perspectives,* ed. Martti Nissinen (Atlanta: Society of Biblical Literature, 2000), 115–146. The author questions Muḥammad's origin in Mecca and wrongly asserts, on page 116, that the term "biblical" in Islamic studies refers generally to Jewish and Christian traditions, including nonbiblical material. He therefore claims that Arabian prophecy was "biblicized" in Yathrib.
22. For a thorough examination of the sources, see Al Makin, *Representing the Enemy: Musaylima in Muslim Literature* (Frankfurt: Peter Lang, 2010).
23. Ibid., 26–36.

4. Ethiopia and Arabia

1. G. W. Bowersock, *The Throne of Adulis* (Oxford: Oxford University Press, 2013).
2. *Periplus Maris Erythraei* 5: The ruler Zôskalês had a good command of Greek.
3. See Chapter 1 in this volume.
4. Qur'ān 53:18–23.
5. I. Shahîd, "The Hijra (Emigration) of the Early Muslims to Abyssinia: The Byzantine

Dimension," in *To Ellênikon: Studies in Honor of Speros Vryonis, Jr.,* ed. J. S. Allen et al. (New Rochelle, NY: Caratzas, 1993), 2:203–213. E. van Donzel and G. Schoeler, "Hiğra," *Encyclopedia Aethiopica,* vol. 3 (Wiesbaden: Harrassowitz, 2007), 30–32.

6. W. Raven, "Some Early Islamic Texts on the Negus of Abyssinia," *Journal of Semitic Studies* 33 (1988): 197–218.
7. Al-Balādhurī, *Ansāb al-Ashrāf,* ed. M. Hamīdullah (Ma'had al Mahkhṭūṭāt: Cairo, 1959), 1:205–206, discussed by Shahīd, "The Hijra," 212n5.
8. See Raven, "Some Early Islamic Texts," 199, for the tears of the *negus,* and 209–214, for Muḥammad's prayer for the *negus* at his death.
9. Stuart Munro-Hay, *Catalogue of the Aksumite Coins in the British Museum* (London: British Museum Press, 1999), 45–46. See also Munro-Hay's articles in *Encyclopedia Aethiopica,* vol. 1 (Wiesbaden: Harrassowitz, 2003), 343, on Armaḥ, and 369–370, on Aṣḥam b. Abğar.
10. The coin is described in Munro-Hay, *Catalogue,* 45, under Armaḥ's silver issues, and it may be seen on plate 55, no. 566. Munro-Hay's speculation may be found in his entry for Armaḥ in the *Encyclopedia Aethiopica.*
11. For these reports, see Raven, "Some Early Islamic Texts," as well as the article "Hiğra," *Encyclopedia Aethiopica,* vol. 3.

12. M. Ḥamīdullah, *Six originaux des Lettres du Prophète de l'Islam: étude paléographique et historique des lettres du Prophète* (Paris: Togui, 1985).
13. Qur'ān 3:45–47. For variant stories in the Islamic tradition, see Raven, "Some Early Islamic Texts," 199–208.
14. Note Qur'ān 3:47: "My Lord, how will I have a child when no man has touched me?" The angel replies to Mary that Allāh creates what he wills: "He only says to it, 'Be,' and it is." Cf. 3:59: "The example of Jesus is like that of Adam. He created him from dust, and then He said, 'Be,' and he was."
15. Texts in Raven, "Some Early Islamic Texts," 207.
16. Ibn Iṣḥaq, *Sīra,* 783–784 (527–528 in Guillaume). For Abraham as neither Jew nor Christian nor pagan, but a *ḥanīf,* see Qur'ān 3:67. See also Chapter 2 in this volume as well as the discussion in G. W. Bowersock, *Empires in Collision in Late Antiquity* (Waltham, MA: Brandeis University Press, 2012), 66–67.
17. See the important doctoral dissertation by Christian Sahner, "Christian Martyrs and the Making of an Islamic Society in the Post-Conquest Period" (PhD diss., Princeton University, 2015).
18. *Kebra Nagast* 84, cf. 114. The standard edition of this work remains that of Carl Bezold, *Abhand-*

lungen der I Kl. der Königlichen Akademie der Wissenschaften 23, Band I (Munich, 1905). The translation history is briefly described in a colophon at the end of the surviving text.

5. *The Persians in Jerusalem*

1. For an exemplary historical analysis of the sources of the *Chronographia* of Theophanes Confessor, with major implications for lost early sources in Greek and Syriac, as preserved in Theophanes as well as in the Arabic history of Agapius, see Maria Conterno, *La "Descrizione dei tempi" all' alba dell' espansione islamica,* Millennium-Studien 47 (Berlin: De Gruyter, 2014).
2. See the path-breaking work of Gideon Avni, *The Byzantine-Islamic Transition in Palestine: An Archaeological Approach* (Oxford: Oxford University Press, 2014).
3. W. E. Kaegi, *Heraclius, Emperor of Byzantium* (Cambridge: Cambridge University Press, 2003).
4. On all this, see G. W. Bowersock, *The Throne of Adulis* (New York: Oxford University Press, 2013).
5. F. Vitto, "Byzantine Mosaics at Bet She'arim: New Evidence for the History of the Site," *'Atiqot* 28 (1996): 115–146; C. J. Robin, "Ḥimyar et Israël," *CRAI* (2004): 831–906, esp. 836, on Ḥimyarite tombs at Bet She'arim.

6. G. W. Nebe and A. Sima, "Die aramäisch / hebräisch / sabäische Grabinschrift der Lea," *Arabian Archaeology and Epigraphy* 15 (2004): 76–83.
7. G. Garitte, *La prise de Jérusalem par les Perses en 614,* CSCO, 202, Georgian text, and 203, Latin translation (Louvain, 1960).
8. Strategios 10.2, in Garitte, *La prise de Jérusalem,* 17–18.
9. Strategios 7.1–3, in Garitte, *La prise de Jérusalem,* 13.
10. Sophronius, *Anacreont.,* no. 14. For the two poems on the holy places of Jerusalem, see text, introduction, and commentary by Herbert Donner, *Die anakreontischen Gedichte Nr. 19 and Nr. 20 des Patriarchen Sophronius von Jerusalem,* Sitzungsber. Heidelberg Akad. Wiss., phil.-hist. Klasse, Bericht 10 (1981).
11. See Chapter 7 in this volume for this episode.
12. H. Cotton et al., eds., *Corpus Inscriptionum Iudaeae / Palestinae* (Berlin: De Gruyter, 2010), 1:36.
13. Gideon Avni, "The Persian Conquest of Jerusalem (614 C.E.)—An Archaeological Assessment," *BASOR* 357 (2010): 35–48.
14. Ibid., 36.
15. Jodi Magness, "A Reexamination of the Archaeological Evidence for the Sasanian Persian Destruction of the Tyropoeon Valley," *BASOR* 287 (1992): 67–74.

16. Robert Schick, *The Christian Communities of Palestine from Byzantine to Islamic Rule* (Princeton, NJ: Darwin Press, 1995), 37–38 and 327–330.
17. Leah Di Segni, "Epigraphic Finds Reveal New Chapters in the History of the Church of the Holy Sepulcher in the Sixth Century," *New Studies on Jerusalem* 12 (2006): 157–163.
18. D. Ben-Ami et al., "New Archaeological and Numismatic Evidence for the Persian Destruction of Jerusalem in 614 CE," *Israel Exploration Journal* 60 (2010): 204–221; G. Bijovsky, "A Single Die Hoard of Heraclius from Jerusalem," *Mélanges Cécile Morrisson, Travaux et Mémoires* (Paris: Collège de France, 2010), 55–92.
19. Clive Foss, "The Persians in the Roman Near East," *Journal of the Royal Asiatic Society*, Series 3, 13 (2003): 149–170.
20. Avni, *The Byzantine-Islamic Transition in Palestine.*

6. Muḥammad and Medina

1. For discussion of these two enigmatic texts, see, most recently, Y. Tobi, "The Jews of Yemen in Light of the Excavation of the Jewish Synagogue in Qanī'," *Proceedings of the Seminar for Arabian Studies* 43 (2013): 349–356. A fundamental survey of Jews in southwestern Arabia is C. J. Robin, "Ḥimyar et Israël," *CRAI* (2004): 831–906.

2. See F. M. Donner, *Muhammad and the Believers at the Origins of Islam* (Cambridge, MA: Harvard University Press, 2010), 34–35. For a thorough review of the Jewish communities in Arabia, see "Quel judaïsme en Arabie?," in *Le judaïsme de l'Arabie antique, Actes du colloque de Jérusalem (février 2006),* ed. C. J. Robin (Turnhout: Brepols, 2015), 15–295, and for the northern Ḥijāz, see 162.
3. For this history, see G. W. Bowersock, *The Throne of Adulis* (New York: Oxford University Press, 2013).
4. Isabel Toral-Niehoff, *Al-Ḥīra: Eine arabische Kulturmetropole im spätantiken Kontext* (Leiden: Brill, 2014), 157–158.
5. Michael Lecker, "The Goal of the Khazraj in the Battle of Bu'āth," in "Were the Ghassānids and the Byzantines behind Muḥammad's *hijra?,*" in *Les Jafnides: Des rois arabes au service de Byzance,* ed. D. Genequand and C. J. Robin, vol. 17 of *Orient et Méditerranée* (Paris: De Boccard, 2015), 278–279.
6. S. A. Arjomand, "The Constitution of Medina: A Sociolegal Interpretation of Muhammad's Acts of Foundation of the *Umma,*" *Int. Jour. Middle East Studies* 41 (2009): 555–575.
7. Lecker "Were the Ghassānids?," 277–293.
8. On this phylarch and the palm groves, see Procop., *De Bellis* 1.19.8–13. Abū Karib has turned up in the newly discovered Petra Papyri: *The Petra Papyri IV,* ed. A. Arjava et al. (Amman: ACOR, 2011), pap.

no. 39, ll. 165 and 488, with commentary on 90 (for line 165).

9. Ibn al-Isḥāq, *Sīrat rasūl Allāh: The Life of Muhammad*, trans. A. Guillaume (Oxford: Oxford University Press, 1955), 499–503, 740–746.

7. Interregnum of the Four Caliphs

1. The interregnum to which this chapter is devoted was thoroughly examined, although from an evidently Shiʿite perspective, by Wilferd Madelung in *The Succession to Muhammad* (Cambridge: Cambridge University Press, 1997). S. J. Shoemaker has explored hints that Muḥammad may not have died in 632 in *The Death of a Prophet* (Philadelphia: University of Pennsylvania Press, 2012).
2. Thomas Presbyter in *Chronica Minora* (Brooks) II. 1. 147–148: *ṭayyāyē d-mḥmt. Doctrina Iacobi nuper Baptizati* 5. 16: ὁ προφήτης ἀνεφάνη ἐρχόμενος μετὰ τῶν Σαρακηνῶν.
3. al-Ṭabarī, *Ta'rīkh,* ed. de Goeje et al. vol. 1, 1794–1795.
4. M. Piccirillo, *L'Arabia Cristiana* (Milan: Jaca, 2002), 219–223.
5. On Caesarea, see Gideon Avni, *The Byzantine-Islamic Transition in Palestine: An Archaeological Approach* (Oxford: Oxford University Press, 2014), 45–48. On Theophanes, see Maria Conterno, *La "descrizione dei tempi" all'alba dell'espansione islamica,* Millennium Studien 47 (Berlin: De Gruyter, 2014);

and "L'abominio della desolazione nel luogo santo: l'ingresso di 'Umar I a Gerusalemme nella Cronografia di Teofane Confessore in tre cronache siriache," in *Luoghi del desiderio: Gerusalemme medievale,* Quaderni di storia religiosa (Verona: Cierre, 2010).

6. S. Bashear, "Qibla Musharriqa and Early Muslim Prayer in Churches," *The Muslim World* 81 (1991): 267–280.
7. Theophanes Confessor, *Chronographia,* ed. De Boor I–II (Leipzig: Teubner, 1883–1885), 1:339; *The Chronicle of Theophanes Confessor,* trans. C. Mango and R. Scott (Oxford: Clarendon Press, 1997), 471–472.
8. Dan. 11.31, with Matt. 24.15 and Mark 13.14.
9. Agapius, *Kitāb al-'unwān,* ed. A. Vasiliev, *Patrol. Oriental.* 11.1, 475. On 945 as the *terminus ante* for Agapius, see Maria Conterno, *La "descrizione dei tempi,"* 123n58; Michael the Syrian, *Chronique,* ed. Chabot (Paris, 1924), 4:419–420 (Syriac); and *Chronicon* of 1234, ed. Chabot et al., CSCO 81, *Scriptores Syri* 36, 199–200.
10. Conterno, *La "descrizione dei tempi,"* together with "L'abominio della desolazione nel luogo santo," 9–24. For the traditional view of Theophilus of Edessa, see R. Hoyland, *Theophilus of Edessa: Chronicle* (Liverpool: Liverpool University Press, 2011).

11. PERF (Archduke Rainer Collection) no. 558. For photograph, transcription, and translation of, and commentary on, the papyrus, see http://www.islamic-awareness.org/History/Islam/Papyri/PERF558.html.
12. For a good discussion of the situation, see B. Sadeghi and M. Goudarzi, "Ṣan'ā' 1 and the Origins of Islam," *Der Islam* 87 (2010): 1–129; as well as F. Déroche on the early codex of which leaves are in Paris and St. Petersburg, "The Codex Parisino-petropolitanus and the *ḥijāzī* Scripts," in the Supplement to the *Proceedings of the Seminar for Arabian Studies*, vol. 40, *The Development of Arabic As a Written Language*, ed. M. C. A. Macdonald (Oxford: Archaeopress, 2010), 113–120.
13. Saïd Nuseibeh and Oleg Grabar, *The Dome of the Rock* (New York: Rizzoli, 1996), 78.
14. This was the word P. K. Hitti used in 1937 in his classic *History of the Arabs* (London: Macmillan, 1937), 182.
15. Gideon Avni is definitive on this in *The Byzantine-Islamic Transition in Palestine*. On the coinage, see Clive Foss, *Arab-Byzantine Coins: An Introduction, with a Catalogue of the Dumbarton Oaks Collection* (Washington, DC: Dumbarton Oaks, 2008).

8. A New Dispensation

1. For the these upheavals, see G. W. Bowersock, "Le tre Rome," *Studi Storici* 47 (2006): 977–991.
2. See Chapter 7 in this volume, together with the fundamental study by Gideon Avni, *The Byzantine-Islamic Transition in Palestine: An Archaeological Approach* (Oxford: Oxford University Press, 2014). For a recent study of early Islamic sites in central Jordan, where again there is no substantive change from the pre-Islamic period, see Bethany Walker, "The Islamization of Central Jordan in the 7th–9th Centuries: Lessons Learned from Hisbān," *Jerusalem Studies in Arabic and Islam* 40 (2013): 143–175, esp. 164: "The town appears to have remained an important ecclesiastical center well into the eighth century C.E."
3. Maria Conterno, *La "descrizione dei tempi" all'alba dell'espansione islamica: un' indagine sulla storiografia greca, siriaca e araba fra VII e VIII secolo* (Berlin: De Gruyter, 2014). As indicated in the Chapter 7, this work demolishes Theophilus of Edessa as a Syriac source for Theophanes and uncovers nearly contemporary Greek and Arabic sources from which the Syriac tradition derived.
4. *The Armenian History Attributed to Sebeos*, 2 vols., trans. R. W. Thomson, comm. James Howard-Johnston (Liverpool: Liverpool University Press, 1999).

5. The papyri from Nessana are a prime example of the use of Greek in this period: *Excavations at Nessana,* vol. 3 of *Non-literary Papyri,* ed. C. J. Kramer Jr. (Princeton, NJ: Princeton University Press, 1958). For the coins, see Clive Foss, *Arab-Byzantine Coins: An Introduction, with a Catalogue of the Dumbarton Oaks Collection* (Washington, DC: Dumbarton Oaks, 2008).
6. Chase F. Robinson, *'Abd al-Malik* (Oxford: Oneworld, 2005), 31–48.
7. Ibid., 50.
8. See Foss, *Arab-Byzantine Coins,* esp. 109–111, on the end of the Arab-Byzantine coinage.
9. Robinson, *'Abd al-Malik,* 95–100.

9. The Dome of the Rock

1. See the extensive introduction and magnificent photographs in Saïd Nuseibeh and Oleg Grabar, *The Dome of the Rock* (New York: Rizzoli, 1996). For a masterly account of the building and its history by a scholar who devoted a lifetime to studying it, see Oleg Grabar, *The Dome of the Rock* (Cambridge, MA: Harvard University Press, 2006).
2. I am deeply grateful to Peter Brown for drawing my attention to this important text, which is now conveniently and reliably accessible in the edition of Denis Meehan, *Adomnán's De Locis Sanctis* (Dublin: Dublin Institute for Advanced Studies, 1958).

3. Thomas O'Loughlin started all this with his article "The Exegetical Purpose of Adomnán's *De Locis Sanctis*," *Cambridge Medieval Celtic Studies* 24 (1992): 37–53, and pursued the argument in subsequent works, notably his book *Adomnán and the Holy Places: The Perceptions of an Insular Monk on the Locations of the Biblical Drama* (London: T. & T. Clark, 2007), for which the review by R. Aist in *Bulletin of the Anglo-Israel Archaeological Society* 26 (2008) represented a turning back of the revisionist tide.
4. Robert Hoyland and Sarah Waidler, "Adomnán's *De Locis Sanctis* and the Seventh-Century Near East," *English Historical Review* 129 (2014): 787–807.
5. The Jerusalem mosque mentioned in this sura cannot have been the mosque that is known today as the al-Aqsa mosque. The text is referring generically to the most remote mosque at the time of the revelation.
6. For this complex tradition, see Oleg Grabar, *The Shape of the Holy: Early Islamic Jerusalem* (Princeton, NJ: Princeton University Press, 1996), 113–114.
7. "Chronicle of 1234, drawing from the lost work of Dionysius of Tel-Maḥrē," in A. Palmer and S. Brock, *The Seventh Century in West-Syrian Chronicles* (Liverpool: Liverpool University Press, 1993), 162.
8. For Arabic inscriptions at Shivta with early quotations from the Qur'ān, see Bilha Moor, "Mosque and Church: Arabic Inscriptions from

Shivta in the Early Islamic period," *Jerusalem Studies in Arabic and Islam* 40 (2013): 73–111, who describes a corpus of Quranic verses "second only to the Umayyad Dome of the Rock in Jerusalem" (76).

9. Grabar, *The Shape of the Holy*, 63–64. On pages 184–186 of this volume Grabar provides the Arabic texts from the inner and outer faces of the octagon as well as those on the east and north doors.
10. Ibid., 63.
11. Verse 33 in the canonical text of the Qur'ān gives these words in the first person as the words of Jesus himself.
12. These appear as the words of Jesus both here and in the Qur'ān.
13. Qur'ān 9:33 and 61:9.
14. See Moshe Halbertal, *Maimonides: Life and Thought* (Princeton, NJ: Princeton University Press, 2013); and G. W. Bowersock, review of *The Story of the Jews*, by S. Schama, *New York Review of Books* 61, no. 7 (April 24, 2014): 41–43.

SELECT BIBLIOGRAPHY

The following list by no means comprises all the documentation in the notes, but it is intended to provide a guide to the most pertinent books. To avoid inconvenient cross-referencing over various chapters, full references to the various articles and books that are cited in the notes are repeated in each chapter.

al-Azmeh, Aziz. *The Emergence of Islam in Late Antiquity: Allāh and His People.* Cambridge: Cambridge University Press, 2014.

Avni, Gideon. *The Byzantine-Islamic Transition in Palestine: An Archaeological Approach.* Oxford: Oxford University Press, 2014.

Bowersock, G. W. *The Throne of Adulis.* New York: Oxford University Press, 2013.

Conterno, Maria. *La "Descrizione dei tempi" all' alba dell' espansione islamica. Un' indagine sulla storiografia greca, siriaca e araba fra VII e VIII secolo.* Millennium Studies 47. Berlin: De Gruyter, 2014.

Crone, Patricia. *Meccan Trade and the Rise of Islam.* Princeton, NJ: Princeton University Press, 1987.

Donner, Fred. *Muhammad and the Believers.* Cambridge, MA: Harvard University Press, 2010.

Gajda, Iwona. *Le royaume de Ḥimyar à l'époque monothéiste.* Paris: Académie des Inscriptions et Belles-Lettres, 2009.

Genequand, D., and C. J. Robin, eds. *Les Jafnides: Des rois arabes au service de Byzance.* Paris: De Boccard, 2015.

Grabar, Oleg. *The Shape of the Holy: Early Islamic Jerusalem.* Princeton, NJ: Princeton University Press, 1996.

Hawting, Gerald R. *The Idea of Idolatry and the Emergence of Islam.* Cambridge: Cambridge University Press, 1999.

Hoyland, Robert. *In God's Path: The Arab Conquests and the Creation of an Islamic Empire.* New York: Oxford University Press, 2015.

Makin, Al. *Representing the Enemy: Musaylima in Muslim Literature.* Frankfurt: Peter Lang, 2010.

Payne, Richard E. *A State of Mixture: Christians, Zoroastrians, and Iranian Political Culture in Late Antiquity.* Oakland: University of California Press, 2015.

Robinson, Chase F. *'Abd al-Malik.* Oxford: Oneworld, 2005.

Schick, Robert. *The Christian Communities of Palestine from Byzantine to Islamic Rule.* Princeton, NJ: Darwin Press, 1995.

Toral-Niehoff, Isabel. *Al-Ḥīra: Eine arabische Kulturmetropole im spätantiken Kontext.* Leiden: Brill, 2014.

ACKNOWLEDGMENTS

My debts to friends and colleagues here and abroad reflect both my personal travels and the international environment of the Institute for Advanced Study, where I have been privileged to work. I have chosen to remember separately my precious Institute colleagues, only recently deceased, Oleg Grabar and Patricia Crone, in the final note to the Prologue of this book. Their presence and their ideas constantly enriched the profit that I had every year from visitors to the Institute who were working in both Near Eastern and Graeco-Roman history. Some of my views were included in a lecture at the University of Vienna in October 2015 at the invitation of Bernhard Palme.

I am grateful to two colleagues in Paris, Christian Robin and Leila Nehme, not only for their important publications on Arabian epigraphy, but for their personal support over the years, and for the magnificent photograph of the Ma'rib inscription of Abraha. Michael Macdonald in Oxford has always been forthcoming in assessing ideas of mine, not least about pagan angels. Finbarr Barry Flood's explorations of Ethiopia have contributed inspiration to my research, and his generosity in making his photographs available is represented here by the image of a famous stele in Axum. Paul Yule, who has devoted his life to illuminating the pre-Islamic antiquities of Ẓafār, has persevered, with his Heidelberg team, in Yemeni archaeology despite difficult working conditions. I am just one of many to have gained from this work. To Fabrice Delrieux, who is a Greek numismatist and epigraphist of the first rank, I owe my deepest gratitude for his willingness to create the two maps in this volume. He has honed his cartographic skills while working on coins and inscriptions, and he has unstintingly shared his talents with me and other colleagues.

My two last doctoral students have instructed me through their outstanding research in areas related to this book. Maria Conterno's dissertation in Florence, at the Istituto Italiano di scienze umane, on the alleged Semitic sources for the *Chronographia* of Theophanes Confessor, opened my eyes to modern misconceptions about Theophilus of Edessa. Her work has now been published and is duly registered in the Select Bibliography. At Princeton I had the joy of supervising, together with Michael Cook, a remarkable dissertation by George Hatke on late antique Ethiopian-Arabian interactions, and the publication of his work is eagerly awaited. I am also grateful to Christian Sahner for giving me the opportunity to see his doctoral dissertation on conversions to Christianity in the early Islamic period.

Finally I must express with especial warmth my indebtedness to two eminent and precious friends of many years, Peter Brown and Christopher Jones. Peter has shown a great interest in this project from the moment I began it, and trying to explain what I was doing served to elicit from him consistently arresting ideas, which have guided me in the planning of these chapters. Christopher, as a friend for well over a half a century, has never failed to improve my pages through perceptive observations and searching questions. No historian could ever hope for better interlocutors.

INDEX

Note: Page numbers in *italics* refer to illustrations.